a failed performance

short plays & scenes by daniil kharms

Published by Plays Inverse Press
Pittsburgh, PA
www.playsinverse.com

ISBN-13: 978-0-9997247-0-5

Cover art "Suprematism" (1915) by Kazimir Malevich
Page & cover design by Tyler Crumrine
Printed in the U.S.A.

PLAYS
INVERSE

a failed performance

short plays & scenes by daniil kharms

translated by
c dylan bassett
emma winsor wood

Plays Inverse Press
Pittsburgh, PA
2018

TRANSLATORS' INTRODUCTION 6

SECTION I: LONGER PLAYS 18
Elizaveta Bam 19
Lapa 45
The Story of Zdygr Appr 63

SECTION II: SHORTER PLAYS IN PROSE 72
Untitled (Elena Ivanovna) 73
Untitled (A Name for Ourselves) 75
The Baroness and the Inkstand 77
Untitled (The Guests) 80
A Controversy 83
A Pleay 85
Untitled (Pyotr Mikhailovich) 87
Chop 94
The Hunters 96
Thomas Bobrov and His Wife 99
Untitled (The End of History) 102
The Fall, or, The Knowledge of Good and Evil 103
Disarmed, or, Failed Love 108
Untitled (America) 109
Untitled (The Baron) 113
Pushkin and Gogol 114
A Failed Performance 115
A Duet: Derbantova and Kukushin-Dergunov 116
The Difference in Height Between Husband and Wife 118
Adam and Eve 119
Untitled (Elizabeth and Chestnut) 121
Untitled (Gregory and Simon) 122
Untitled (Nina and Barbara) 124
Leonidov and Grigoriev 126
The Server 127
Evstigneev's Laugh 130
Untitled (Fedya #1) 134
Untitled (Fedya #2) 135
Extensive Research 136

Untitled (Anything Meaningful on Earth) 139
Shameless: An Opera in Four Acts 140
Everyday Happenings: A Vaudeville 141
Grandpa and the Turnip: A Ballet 142
The Interruption 146
Ratsby's Victory 149
The Lecture 152
Makarov and Petersen #3 154
Four Examples: How a New Idea Dumfounds the Unprepared Mind 156

SECTION III: SHORTER PLAYS IN VERSE 158
Temptation 159
Untitled (Doctor Matron) 163
Papa and the Observers 165
Untitled (The Sand) 167
Dinner 169
Joy 171
Water Cooler Chat 176
Gvidon 182
He and Windmill 191
Untitled (He and She) 194
The Window 196
Untitled (Mother and Father) 198
Water and Hnyu 199
Untitled (The Gnostic) 202
The Architect 203
Andrei Semyonovich and the Mathematician 206
Untitled (Nicholas and Alexandra) 208
Untitled (Ryabichkov and the Coffee Pot) 211
The Ball 213
Untitled (The Student) 217
Pyotr and Batov 222
Untitled (The Telegram) 223

TRANSLATORS' INTRODUCTION

C DYLAN BASSETT
EMMA WINSOR WOOD

THE CONTRADICTIONS OF DANIIL KHARMS

"The Server"
A man walks into a restaurant and tries to order the "boeuf-buoy." At first the waiter thinks he's misheard (perhaps he meant "Boeuf Bourguignon"?), but no: boeuf-buoy, boeuf-buoy, boeuf-buoy, boeuf-buoy! "What? Huh?" the waiter asks before eventually giving up and leaving. At that point (in our translation), a second waiter comes in, and the entire, already-repetitive scene repeats.

Daniil Kharms, born Daniil Ivanovich Yuvachev, not only adopted "Kharms" as his pen name, he also changed it officially: his passport read Daniil Kharms. The name is a multifaceted pun on the English words for "charm" and "harm" as well as a nod to Kharms's literary obsession, Sherlock Holmes ("Kholms" in Russian)—a figure he tried to emulate as he walked down St. Petersburg's Nevsky Prospect in a felt hat, puffing a pipe. Kharms was a poet, a playwright, a writer of fiction and short essays, a children's book author, and, ultimately, a pioneer of the hybrid text, which defies exact categorization. Most critics call him an absurdist writer as well as a political one.

"Pushkin and Gogol"
Two canonical Russian writers literally trip over each other, over and over and over and over again.

Kharms was born in December 1905, which means he was eleven when the Russian Revolution began in 1917; eighteen when Stalin came to power; thirty when Stalin began exterminating his own citizens in what has since become known as "the Terror"; thirty-three when he was diagnosed with schizophrenia; thirty-five when he was arrested for spreading "defeatist propaganda"; and thirty-six when he starved to death in the psychiatric ward of a prison hospital, in February 1942, while famine ravaged the city of Leningrad during the German blockade.

Kharms's work, the majority of it unpublished during his lifetime, was preserved by his friend, the philosopher Yakov Semyonovich

Druskin. It did not begin appearing in print in the Soviet Union until the 1960s and 70s. His first major book collection didn't come out until the late 1980s, during Gorbachev's *glasnost*.

"A Pleay"
A man tries to tell his mother that he's getting married. As she continually—perhaps willfully—mishears him, the man becomes increasingly frustrated. Eventually, he strangles her.

In Josef Stalin's Soviet state, people disappeared without explanation. The innocent were believed guilty until proven otherwise. The state took its own citizens hostage and executed thousands based on verdicts made during sham trials. There were famines, wars, freezing winters, the prison of poverty and, with it, the monotony of daily life as a struggle for survival. No one went untouched by this: Kharms's first wife, Esther Rusakova, was sentenced to five years in the Gulag; his close friend, the poet Aleksandr Vvedensky, died shortly after being arrested for "counter-revolutionary agitation" in 1941; the list could go on. In Stalin's Soviet state, ambiguity and visceral violence determined human relations.

Kharms's writing offers us a window into that world: an endless cycle of paranoia, fear, boredom, confusion, a world in which, with the next knock on the door, you could "disappear," a world in which your own government, an entity supposedly tasked with keeping you safe, presented the greatest danger. Thus, in Kharms's writings, reality is not depicted as an onging narrative, the kind so often portrayed in both contemporary and historical Realist fiction or poetry. Reality, for him and for everyone in the Soviet Union at that time, was not rational, not full of meaning, not linear, not ongoing. It was, instead, a network of stoppages and digressions, an endless, repetitive series of pointless interruptions, collisions, misunderstandings, inexplicable acts of violence, disappointments, abrupt endings. Reality was brutal, uncertain, irrational, terrifying—and so is Kharms's writing.

"Disarmed, or, Failed Love"
A man attempts to rape a woman. However, unzipping his pants, prepared to complete the act, he finds he is missing the

essential tool. He gropes his crotch: nothing.

For many political Soviet writers in the 1920s and 30s, art served as social documentation—a record of the material and psychological dimensions of society—and a means of delivering overt political messages. Osip Mandelstam compares Stalin's fingers to worms and his moustache to a cockroach in his "Stalin epigram." In her poem cycle "Requiem," Anna Akhmatova documents the months she stood in line outside of Kresty Prison in Leningrad, waiting for news or a glimpse of her son. The irony of this kind of artistic sociopolitical record-keeping is that it tends to beautify what is abhorrent, to humanize what is monstrous, and—to one degree or another—to render pleasing what is unethical, terrifying, painful. It normalizes that which should not be incorporated into the realm of human experience. Theodor Adorno explains this effect:

> The so-called artistic representation of the sheer physical pain of people . . . contains, however remotely, the power to elicit enjoyment out of it . . . The aesthetic principle of stylization . . . make[s] an unthinkable fate appear to have some meaning; it is transfigured, something of its horror is removed.[1]

What's equally concerning is the way in which Realist political literature tends inadvertently (and ironically) to inhibit our ability to see clearly the subject matter it means to show. It represents the horror of a given event or social context by aesthetic means, thereby taming it—framing it in digestible images. Insistence on describing a thing dilutes its indescribable realities. Indeed, there are things we cannot see, not because they are unclear to us, but because they have been made too clear. Mimesis, then, can have an obfuscating effect that perpetuates the closed epistemological loop between perception and reality.

Kharms, however, seems utterly disinterested in art that monumentalizes actual suffering or directly and unambiguously confronts questions of justice and ethics. Thus, against the decisively

[1] Theodor Adorno, et al., *Aesthetics and Politics*, ed. Ronald Taylor (London: Verso, 1980), 189.

revolutionary Soviet State and the various so-called "counter-revolutionary" movements of anti-government art, Kharms eschews impulses toward either resistance or representation. He refuses to speak out, to take a stand, to make a statement, to participate in political and artistic systems that demand participation. His art is an anti-art—full of boredom, insignificance, tedious repetition, even distasteful and crude shenanigans. This anti-art, like anti-fables or anti-myths, lacks a moral conclusion, emotional catharsis, or even clear political commentary. Kharms's refusal to make committed, didactic, (re)constructive art constitutes a critique of progressive social values. Kharms's most revolutionary act resides precisely in his refusal to join anyone's revolution.

*

At the same time, Kharms's "nonsense" acts as a rhetorical weapon against state-ordered logos, exposing the deterministic ideologies of the time and thus liberating the reader from the oppressive protocols of mandated thought and behavior. Critics and enthusiasts alike have described Kharms in these terms, and have tended to interpret his decision to write in this way—absurdly, nonsensically, bizarrely—as a political one. Under Stalin, Social Realism, a style that depicted a romanticized Soviet reality in straightforward, "accessible" language, was the only accepted form of literature; all other literature was suspicious in the eyes of the state. And so, in this context, it is difficult *not* to read Kharms—who makes up words, moves between verse and prose, balances a simultaneity of conflicting tones, starts and ends *in media res*, portrays the ridiculous as if it were banal and vice versa—as a political writer aiming to undermine the oppressive political forces of his time. In such a reading, Kharms's work is an ethical, subversive, and practical reaction to public life under Stalin, while he himself appears eagerly engaged in the fight for human rights and social justice. In this same frame, Kharms's absurdism serves a political teleology: to enact the emotional and psychological realities of extreme political oppression.

It would be negligent, perhaps even irresponsible, to ignore this reading. After all, Kharms lived and died in fear and poverty as a political victim. Stalin's police, the NKVD, censored, suppressed, publicly humiliated, and arrested Kharms multiples times. After his final arrest, he starved to death in prison. In some ways, we cannot separate Kharms's writing from his experiences. His life demands that we draw political, even moralist, conclusions from his writing. The trope of political victimhood engenders ready-made interpretations from which we extract (for better or for worse) multivalent political parables and coded social commentaries. But, although we can accurately embrace Kharms as a victim and social commentator, we should not limit him to that reading alone.

For we believe that labels like absurd or proto-surrealist, while not inaccurate, oversimplify any reading of Kharms—diminishing the potential power of his work in the process. They not only suggest both unfashionable and purely historical literary practices and movements (Surrealism happened between the 1920s and 1940s, for example), but also imply a writing which is unconcerned with, and disconnected from, "real life." These words make it easy to dismiss Kharms, especially in a contemporary literary climate that values message-driven, political writing. For Kharms, the "absurd" or "nonsensical" was a way *into*, not an *escape from*, reality. For him, the absurd lies at the material foundation of the Real. That is, the nonsensical, the inexplicable, and the otherworldly make up the visceral, often ignored core of life as we know it. Thus, the absurd, paradoxically, presents a means to confront reality on its own terms—a reality too real to be known, a reality which is unbearable, ineffable, chaotic, infinite.

While we don't recommend completely rejecting political or absurdist interpretations of Kharms, we believe such readings allow us to cling to neat political and aesthetic categories, and so dilute much that is shocking, enlivening, and affecting in Kharms. We thus suggest a reading beyond the absurdist label as well as the political motives that appear to come with it—to read these plays not merely as political allegories but as much more than that: as metaphysical, mystical, existential, and philosophical texts that aim to break down the apparent structures of the world (sequential time, space, semantics, scientific facts, etc.). Kharms is often categorized among politically-charged absurdists such as Samuel Beckett, Albert Camus, and Eugène Ionesco. But we might also locate him in a league with religious, psychological thinkers like Fyodor Dostoevsky and Søren Kierkegaard, with materialist philosophers like Martin Heidegger, or with experimental writers like Gertrude Stein.

And, in fact, it's not hard to read Kharms as a Russian mystic, a religious philosopher, a spiritual wanderer obsessed with ancient practices and rituals, writing in order to transform and elevate the human soul. Kharms's anti-logic doesn't enact or perform consciousness, but reconstructs it. The absurd and the existential here are not cultural but theological, not symptomatic but prescriptive, not performative but transformative. The anti-logical is a means to an authentic readerly experience autonomous from "real world" reason or functionality, an experience which ultimately suggests to us that the a-logical—i.e., the supernatural, the ridiculous, the extreme, the uncanny—constitutes not a limit case of human existence, but, rather, a feature inherent to it. Kharms's nonsense encodes the suspicion that the world is stranger and more violent than we can see.

*

Kharms's official career as a literary playwright began and ended in January 1928, when he wrote and produced *Elizaveta Bam*—a play written in a combination of prose and verse that is split into 19 sections, each given a title that indicates a shift in tone or genre. The play, which employs Dada logic and *zaum* (or trans-sense) poetry, was commissioned by the OBERIU, the "Association for Real Art," a group of experimental writers co-founded by Kharms, and performed during "Three Left Hours," a lengthy event which also showcased poetry, film, and jazz. While *Elizaveta Bam* has become one of the most celebrated and important works of the OBERIU, it was widely disliked and disregarded at the time of its initial production. One reviewer called the play "undisguised cynicism, complete chaos in which no one could understand anything at all." The fact that the play lacked Socialist values and political relevance brought Kharms and his associates negative attention. From this point forward Kharms was labeled, both by the state and by the tastemakers of the time, a nuisance and a threat to industrialization and Socialist progress. While Kharms would go on to write many plays after *Elizaveta Bam*, none would ever reach the stage.

*

Kharms's drama is a meta-drama; it not only documents the emotional narratives of our lives, but also exposes the failure of theater as a universal narrative form. In the "OBERIU Manifesto," we read:

> If an actor who portraying a government minister on stage starts walking around on all fours and howling like a wolf, or if an actor portraying a Russian peasant suddenly recites a long speech in Latin, that's theater, it will interest the spectator, even if it occurs without any relation to a dramatic plot. It will be an isolated moment: a series of such moments, organized by the director, creates a theatrical performance... This is the kind of plot that only theater can offer. The plot of the theatrical performance is theatrical just as the plot of a musical work is musical. They both represent the same thing, the world of phenomena, but depending on the material, they communicate it differently, each in its own way.[2]

For Kharms and the OBERIU, theater should produce pure theatricality. Theater should exist for theater's sake. The project of the OBERIU therein is twofold: 1) to upset the traditions and expectations of formal theater, and 2) to collapse the distinctions between theater and ordinary life. (By all accounts, Kharms saw no difference between theatrical performance and daily activity—on occasion, in his trademark Sherlock Holmes get-up, he danced in the streets reciting poems.) Thus the theater does not encapsulate human experience, but disrupts it—freeing singular experiences from their constituted, universalizing wholes. In this way, Kharms transcends drama by refusing to monumentalize human experience.

[2] Daniil Kharms, *I Am a Phenomenon Quite Out of the Ordinary: The Notebooks, Diaries and Letters of Daniil Kharms*, trans. and ed. by Anthony Anemone and Peter Scotto (Boston: Academic Studies Press, 2013), 163.

The result is a drama "beyond" drama.

This "beyond" is often corporeal; Kharms is obsessed with involuntary bodily outbursts—hiccups, burps, stutters, snorts, snores, and vomit. These outbursts sound like speech, and yet, they cannot be interpreted as such—and so expose the limitations of language. Suspending the human voice, they approximate that which is "beyond" communication.

*

Previous translators have thoroughly documented the difficulties (even impossibilities) of translating Kharms: not only does his translator face a plethora of logical and grammatical inconsistencies (what Kharms called "slight errors"), the translator must also wrangle with word play, pun, neologism, nonce words, witticism, innuendo, jokes, allusions, and ambiguities. But, above all, Kharms is difficult to translate in part because he uses language not as an epistemological apparatus or means of signification, but as an object, a pure artistic material. In 1933, he writes that literature is:

> no longer simply words and thoughts printed on paper, but a thing just as real as the crystal inkwell standing before me on the desk. It seems this poem, which has become a thing, can be taken from the paper and thrown at the window, and the window will shatter. That's what the words can do![3]

Here, Kharms announces his foremost project: to rid literature of its metaphorical properties and to grant language an autonomous ontological stature. Against the assumption of signification, Kharms attempts to make language wholly somatic, to liberate the materiality of language from the limitations of its supposed meaning. Language becomes a physical endeavor, a constructive practice, a brick to throw through the "window." Kharms thus presents language as material in flux. Consider the following scene from *Elizaveta Bam*:

> **MOMMY:** *(chasing after ELIZAVETA BAM)* Do you eat wheat?

[3] Kharms, *I Am a Phenomenon*, 416.

ELIZAVETA BAM: Do you eat peas?

DADDY: Do you eat meat? *(Running.)*

MOMMY: Do you eat seeds?

IVAN IVANOVICH: Do you eat beets? *(Starts running.)*

ELIZAVETA BAM: Do you eat sheep?

DADDY: Do you eat beef?

In this excerpt, language fails to produce, understand, preserve, or communicate anything outside of itself. Instead, it enacts its own reality. Kharms destabilizes conventional methods of cognitive and communicative forms and employs words according to phonetic and etymological properties. Thus, he highlights the material quality of individual sounds. Peas becomes meat becomes seeds becomes beets, and so on—while the repeated "eat" emphasizes the central "ee" sound of those nouns. Through this evolution of sounds, which, in this piece and throughout the book, we have prioritized over literal, one-to-one translations, Kharms renders language as an evolving landscape in which anything and everything might appear. By these means, Kharms enshrines ongoing metamorphoses and permutations for us to witness. His plays showcase a state of change, so that beneath the level of meaning and interpretation, we experience dramatic forms in and of themselves as they clash, interrupt, echo, and transform into each other.

In short: facing all of the complexities in Kharms's language, it is not enough to simply translate *what* a given word means, but to consider *how* that word functions with or against the words around it. To translate Kharms is to account for the various (ever-changing) language games that produce writing itself. The translator of Kharms must also act as interpreter, commentator, editor, critic, and co-writer.

This is especially true of the "plays" and "scenes" included in this book. In fact, we acknowledge that Kharms himself might have rejected those terms altogether—after all, his writing is resolutely anti-genre. The term "play" seems to connote something more stable—more permanent, durational, and concrete—than anything we find in Kharms. Though the longer works were certainly intentionally crafted as plays, Kharms might have called many of the shorter pieces "events," "chances," "happenings," "coincidences," or even "accidents." The temporary, or "accidental," essence of these dialogue-driven texts is clear when one encounters them in their "natural habitat"—Kharms's notebooks. There, they are situated as part of an interconnected patchwork of drafts, journal entries, diagrams, poems, and notes. Thus, while we have maintained as best we could the irregularities found in Kharms's original, and mostly handwritten, manuscripts—missing stage directions, inconsistent punctuation and capitalization, etc.—we have occasionally standardized the formatting of individual texts so as to provide clarity to actors, directors, and readers alike.

In this volume, we labored to preserve the mood, the playfulness, the formal structures (or the lack thereof), and the jolt of alterity in each individual work. Indeed, more conventional, literal-minded translators may find "errors" and "inaccuracies" in our translation; at times, we sacrificed literal translations in order to maintain original tones, emotional textures, rhyme, formal patterns, and word play. For instance, in the previous excerpt from *Elizaveta Bam*, a more direct translator might have translated "sheep" as "mutton" (*baranina*) and "wheat" as "flour" (*muka*). However, in order to preserve the original assonance of the sequence, we changed these words slightly. From time to time, we also repeated words, clauses, sentences, or, in the case of *The Server* entire scenes in order to enact the paranoia, fear, frenzy, or tedium inherent in the original Russian versions. We have also anglicized some words and names to highlight their many valences in Russian, and we have, in some cases, played up colloquialisms and profanity, to emphasize the alterity of the text at the time it was written. Above all else, we have endeavored to render into English the only Kharms we know—impossible, baffling, hilarious, dark, authentic, honest—and to do so in a way that makes him readable and exciting, not just to the student of Russian literature but to any interested reader.

In *Negotiations*, Gilles Deleuze discusses the advantages and pitfalls of interpreting, translating, or collaborating with authors of the past. He argues that, in our collaborations, we must attend to the author's "shifting, slipping, dislocations, and hidden emissions" in order to create "a child that would be his own offspring, yet monstrous."[4] To translate Kharms is not to reconstruct him into English, but to actualize his monstrous offspring. At this stage in history, there are many "monstrous" translations of Kharms in the world. We hope, in some small way, ours—the first volume dedicated to his plays in English—will contribute to Kharms's legacy as a playwright, and also to the history and production of theater more broadly.

A note on reading the text: We have ordered the plays in this collection into three generic sections: Longer Plays, Shorter Plays in Prose, and Shorter Plays in Verse. Within each section, we have placed individual texts in chronological order—corresponding either to the dates Kharms wrote beneath them (along with the occasional dedication, signature, or place name), or, for undated plays, the dates scholars now attribute to them. Where no consensus is available, we've grouped plays alongside others of similar style or subject.

---

[4] Gilles Deleuze, *Negotiations, 1972-1990*, trans. by Martin Joughin (New York: Columbia University Press, 1995), 6.

SECTION I: LONGER PLAYS

ELIZAVETA BAM

(A small, shallow, simple room.)

1. A REALIST MELODRAMA

ELIZAVETA BAM: Right now. Any minute now. Any second. The door will open and they'll come in… They'll come in. They'll catch me. They'll take me away. Oh god. *(Whispering.)* What have I done! What have I done? If only I had known… Run away! Run? Run where? The door leads to the stairs, they'll find me on the stairs. They're waiting for me on the stairs. They're on the stairs where else could they be! I could go through the window! *(Looks at the window.)* I can't reach it. Can't reach. What should I do? I can't. I hear their footsteps. It's them. I hear them. Their footsteps. I'll lock the door. I won't let them in. Let them knock forever. I won't answer. *(Locks the door.)*

(A knock at the door, a VOICE offstage.)

FIRST VOICE: Elizaveta Bam, let us in. *(Pause.)* Bam, open up.

SECOND VOICE: What's she doing in there? Why won't she let us in?

FIRST VOICE: She'll let us in. Elizaveta Bam, open up.

(*ELIZAVETA BAM throws herself across the bed and covers her ears. VOICES speak from the distance.*)

FIRST VOICE: Elizaveta Bam, open this door!

SECOND VOICE: *(Whispering.)* Tell her if she doesn't let us in, we'll break down the door. Wait, let me try. *(Tries.)*

FIRST VOICE: *(Yelling.)* We'll break down the door ourselves if you don't let us in!

SECOND VOICE: *(Whispering.)* Maybe she isn't here.

FIRST VOICE: *(Whispering.)* She's here. Where else would she be? She ran right up the stairs. This is the only door here. She has nowhere else to go. *(Yells.)* Elizaveta Bam, I won't say it again.

(ELIZAVETA BAM sits upright.)

Open the door. *(Pause.)* OK. Break it down!

FIRST & SECOND VOICE: *(Trying to break down the door.)* Bam Bam Bam Bam Bam Bam.

(ELIZAVETA BAM runs around the room. One of them rams into the door.)

SECOND VOICE: Do you have a knife on you?

(ELIZAVETA BAM presses her ear against the door.)

FIRST VOICE: Put your shoulder into it.

SECOND VOICE: It won't budge. I'll try again. Hold on. (*Tries to break down the door with his shoulder.)*

(The door cracks but won't break.)

ELIZAVETA BAM: I'll open the door if you tell me what you're going to do to me.

(They stop banging.)

FIRST VOICE: You know what we're going to do to you.

ELIZAVETA BAM: No, I don't know. You're going to kill me?

FIRST VOICE: You need to be punished.

SECOND VOICE: You won't get away.

ELIZAVETA BAM: Can you at least tell me how I'm guilty.

FIRST VOICE: You know how.

ELIZAVETA BAM: I don't.

FIRST VOICE: You do.

ELIZAVETA BAM: *(Stomping.)* Don't.

FIRST VOICE: Sorry, we don't believe you.

SECOND VOICE: You're a criminal.

ELIZAVETA BAM: Ha-ha-ha-ha! And you think you can kill me with a clean conscience?

(Again she runs around the room.)

FIRST VOICE: We'll kill you precisely because of our conscience.

ELIZAVETA BAM: You have no conscience.

2. A REALIST COMEDY

SECOND VOICE: What do you mean, no conscience? Pyotr Nikolayevich, she's saying we have no conscience.

ELIZAVETA BAM: You have no conscience, Ivan Ivanovich. You're a con man. (*She puts her hands on her hips and drives her head into the door.*)

SECOND VOICE: Who's a con man? Me? Me? Me? I'm the con man?

FIRST VOICE: Hold on a minute, Ivan Ivanovich. Elizaveta Bam, I order you—

SECOND VOICE: No, hold on, Pyotr Nikolayevich, so you think I'm a fraudster? Benedict Arnold!

FIRST VOICE: Forget about it.

SECOND VOICE: No, hold on, tell me what you really think—you think I'm a crook?

FIRST VOICE: Yes, you're a fraud!

SECOND VOICE: Oh, so in your opinion, I'm a con man? Is that what you're saying?

(ELIZAVETA BAM runs around the room.)

FIRST VOICE: Go to hell, clown! Here you are on this important case. Someone says one word to you and you're up a wall. What does that make you? A basic idiot!

SECOND VOICE: And you're a fraud.

FIRST VOICE: Go to hell!

ELIZAVETA BAM: Ivan Ivanovich is a con man!

SECOND VOICE: I'll never forgive you for this.

FIRST VOICE: I'll throw you down the stairs.

(ELIZAVETA BAM opens the door. IVAN IVANOVICH is on crutches. PYOTR NIKOLAYEVICH is sitting down wrapped in bandages.)

IVAN IVANOVICH: Go ahead and try.

PYOTR NIKOLAYEVICH: Watch me! Watch!

IVAN IVANOVICH: You don't have the stomach for it.

PYOTR NIKOLAYEVICH: You don't think I have a stomach?

IVAN IVANOVICH & ELIZAVETA BAM: You don't!

IVAN IVANOVICH: You don't! You don't! He doesn't. You mean him, right? *(Points to PYOTR NIKOLAYEVICH.)* Tell him!

ELIZAVETA BAM: He doesn't.

PYOTR NIKOLAYEVICH: Elizaveta Bam, you can't talk to me that way.

ELIZAVETA BAM: Who?

PYOTR NIKOLAYEVICH: You have no voice. You committed a crime. You can't say that kind of thing to me. You're a criminal.

ELIZAVETA BAM: Why?

PYOTR NIKOLAYEVICH: Why what?

ELIZAVETA BAM: Why am I the criminal?

PYOTR NIKOLAYEVICH: Because your voice has been taken away.

IVAN IVANOVICH: You're deprived of a voice.

ELIZAVETA BAM: I'm not deprived! Check your watch and see for yourself.

(PYOTR NIKOLAYEVICH and IVAN IVANOVICH walk through the door into the room.)

3. ABSURDLY COMEDIC AND NAIVE SCENE

PYOTR NIKOLAYEVICH: That won't be necessary. I've stationed guards at the door and, at the slightest interruption, Ivan Ivanovich will turn to the side and hiccup.

ELIZAVETA BAM: Oh, show me, please! Show me!

PYOTR NIKOLAYEVICH: Ok, watch. Turn around.

(PYOTR NIKOLAYEVICH walks downstage. IVAN IVANOVICH follows him. PYOTR NIKOLAYEVICH taps on a stool. One. Two. Three. IVAN IVANOVICH hiccups loudly and upends the stool.)

ELIZAVETA BAM: Show me again. Please.

(They repeat the trick. PYOTR NIKOLAYEVICH walks downstage. Again he taps the stool. IVAN IVANOVICH hiccups loudly and upends the stool.)

ELIZAVETA BAM: How did you do that?

PYOTR NIKOLAYEVICH: It's easy. Show her, Ivan!

IVAN IVANOVICH: I'd love to. Watch. *(He gets down on all fours and kicks up one leg.)*

ELIZAVETA BAM: Wonderful! *(Shouting.)* Mommy! Come over here! These magicians are performing. My Mommy is on her way… Allow me to introduce Pyotr Nikolayevich and Ivan Ivanovich! Will you show us another trick?

IVAN IVANOVICH: Sure thing.

PYOTR NIKOLAYEVICH: Alley-oop! Here we go! We're really going.

(IVAN IVANOVICH tries to stand on his head but falls over.)

(MOMMY and DADDY enter. They sit on the floor and watch.)

IVAN IVANOVICH: *(Also sitting on the floor.)* There's nowhere to sit.

ELIZAVETA BAM: Do you want a towel?

IVAN IVANOVICH: Why would I want a towel?

ELIZAVETA BAM: *(Giggling.)* Just because.

IVAN IVANOVICH: You're nice to look at.

ELIZAVETA BAM: Why do you say that?

IVAN IVANOVICH: Um-um-um-um-um because *(Hiccups loudly.)* you're a forget-me-not.

ELIZAVETA BAM: A forget-me-not? Well *(In a nasally voice.)* you're a tulip.

IVAN IVANOVICH: A what?

ELIZAVETA BAM: Tulip.

IVAN IVANOVICH: *(Confused.)* Very well, Sir.

ELIZAVETA BAM: *(Through her nose.)* Allow me to pluck you.

DADDY: *(In a deep voice.)* Elizaveta, don't be stupid.

ELIZAVETA BAM: *(To DADDY, in a high voice.)* Yes, right away, Daddy, right away, I'm done. *(She sits down on a root and speaks to IVAN IVANOVICH through her nose.)* Get on your hands and knees.

(MOMMY is unimpressed. She walks to the front of the stage, frowning.)

IVAN IVANOVICH: If you'll excuse me please, Elizaveta Cockroachovna, I need to go home. My wife is waiting for me. She has many children, Elizaveta Cockroachovna. Forgive me for bothering you. Forgive me. I'm the type of person that gets kicked out wherever I go. For what, you ask? Am I a thief or something? No, Elizaveta Edwardson, I'm an honest man. I have a wife at home. My wife has children. Good kids, too. Each one of them carries a matchbox in their mouth. So forgive me, Elizaveta Michaelson, I need to go home now.

(IVAN IVANOVICH puts on a winter coat and leaves. ELIZAVETA BAM ties a rope to one of MOMMY'S legs and then wraps the other end of the rope around the chair. No one speaks.)

MOMMY: *(Singing to music.)*

Behold the day erupts.
The water burns red

the seagull soars over the lake, etc. etc.

(MOMMY finishes singing. She walks around the room, dragging the chair behind her.)

PYOTR NIKOLAYEVICH: Here we are.

DADDY: Praise God. *(Exits.)*

4. A REALISTIC COMEDY, ORDINARY LIFE

ELIZAVETA BAM: Mommy, would you like to go for a walk?

MOMMY: Um. Do you want to go for a walk?

ELIZAVETA BAM: Obviously!

MOMMY: I'm not going.

ELIZAVETA BAM: Let's go, ple-e-e-ease.

MOMMY: OK. Let's go.

(They exit with chair. The stage is empty.)

(A pause.)

5. RHYTHM OF THE SOUL

(Enter IVAN IVANOVICH and PYOTR NIKOLAYEVICH.)

IVAN IVANOVICH & PYOTR NIKOLAYEVICH:
Where, where, where
is Bam,
is Bam,
is Bam,

PYOTR NIKOLAYEVICH: Here, here, here.

IVAN IVANOVICH: There, there, there.

(IVAN IVANOVICH and PYOTR NIKOLAYEVICH speak in accentual verse.)

PYOTR NIKOLAYEVICH:
Where are we?

IVAN IVANOVICH:
We're locked up with no key.

PYOTR NIKOLAYEVICH:
Another tra-ge-dy…
Please don't bother me!

IVAN IVANOVICH:
Enough rhyme.
It's almost time.

(Both in singsong.)

PYOTR NIKOLAYEVICH: Where is Elizaveta Bam?

IVAN IVANOVICH: What do you want with her?

PYOTR NIKOLAYEVICH: I want to kill her!

IVAN IVANOVICH: Hmmm, looks like Elizaveta Bam is sitting on a bench over there.

PYOTR NIKOLAYEVICH: Let's get over there. Hurry!

(They run in place. A log is brought to the front of the stage and sawed into pieces as they speak. They continue running.)

PYOTR NIKOLAYEVICH & IVAN IVANOVICH:
Hop, hop,
on your feet
the sun falls
behind the hills
in pink clouds
soft, soft
from a locomotive
the owl hoots
hoot, hoot—
stop, stop.
The log is fully sawed.

6. THE DAILY GRIND

(The side wing withdraws. Elizaveta Bam is sitting on a bench.)

ELIZAVETA BAM: Are you looking for me?

PYOTR NIKOLAYEVICH: There you are! Look, Vanka, there she is!

IVAN IVANOVICH: Where, where, where.

PYOTR NIKOLAYEVICH: Over here, under the whatchamacallit.

(A BEGGAR enters.)

IVAN IVANOVICH: Drag her out!

PYOTR NIKOLAYEVICH: She won't budge.

BEGGAR: *(To ELIZAVETA BAM.)* Comrade, help me.

IVAN IVANOVICH: *(Stuttering.)* Next time I will have more experience. In fact, I've been paying attention to everything. I'll be ready next time.

ELIZAVETA BAM: *(To BEGGAR.)* I have nothing.

BEGGAR: Not even a penny?

ELIZAVETA BAM: Why don't you ask that guy over there. *(Points to PYOTR NIKOLAYEVICH.)*

(A table emerges on stage. ELIZAVETA BAM pushes her chair up to the table and sits.)

PYOTR NIKOLAYEVICH: *(To IVAN IVANOVICH, stuttering.)* Watch what you're doing!

IVAN IVANOVICH: *(Stuttering.)* I'm digging up roots.

BEGGAR: Help me, comrades.

PYOTR NIKOLAYEVICH: *(To the BEGGAR.)* Come on then. Climb down there.

IVAN IVANOVICH: Get your hands on the ground.

(BEGGAR gets on all fours.)

PYOTR NIKOLAYEVICH: Don't worry, he knows the drill.

ELIZAVETA BAM: Why don't you sit down, too. Don't be so traditional.

(Pause.)

IVAN IVANOVICH: I thank you, sir.

PYOTR NIKOLAYEVICH: *(Sitting down.)* Let's sit.

(Pause. They eat soup. Silence)

ELIZAVETA BAM: Why isn't my husband here? I wonder where he is? Why isn't he here?

PYOTR NIKOLAYEVICH: He'll be here. *(He jumps up and begins to run around the stage.)* Abracadabra.

IVAN IVANOVICH: Ha-ha-ha. *(He jumps up and runs directly toward PYOTR NIKOLAYEVICH.)* Where's home base?

ELIZAVETA BAM: Right here, behind this line.

PYOTR NIKOLAYEVICH: *(Tags IVAN IVANOVICH.)* You're it!

(DADDY comes on stage holding a pen and quill.)

ELIZAVETA BAM: Ivan Ivanovich, run over here.

IVAN IVANOVICH: Ha-ha-ha! I have no legs!

(He has no legs.)

PYOTR NIKOLAYEVICH: Crawl then!

DADDY: *(Addresses the audience.)* Here is she about whom it is written!

ELIZAVETA BAM: Who's it?

IVAN IVANOVICH: It's me, ha-ha-ha, the one wearing pants!

PYOTR NIKOLAYEVICH & ELIZAVETA BAM: Ha-ha-hahahah!

DADDY: Copernicus was the greatest scientist.

IVAN IVANOVICH: There's hair on my head!

PYOTR NIKOLAYEVICH & ELIZAVETA BAM: Ha-ha-ha-ha-ha-ha-ha!

IVAN IVANOVICH: I'm lying directly on the floor! The floor and I are one.

(Enter MOMMY.)

PYOTR NIKOLAYEVICH & ELIZAVETA BAM: Ha! Ha! Ha! Ha! Ha!

ELIZAVETA BAM: Stop, stop, I can't take it! I can't!

DADDY: If you buy a bird, make sure it has teeth. If it has teeth, it's not a bird. *(Exits.)*

7. SERIOUS MELODRAMA DIRECTLY FROM THE SOURCE

PYOTR NIKOLAYEVICH: *(Raising his hand.)* Listen to me, I beg you. I want to prove to you that suffering is random. When I was still a young man, I lived in a small house with a squeaky door. I lived alone. There were only mice and cockroaches. Cockroaches everywhere. Each night, I locked the door and turned off the lamp. I slept. I feared nothing.

VOICE OFFSTAGE: Nothing.

MOMMY: Nothing.

FLUTE OFFSTAGE: !—!.

IVAN IVANOVICH: Nothing.

PIANO: !—!.

PYOTR NIKOLAYEVICH: Nothing! *(Pause.)* I promise there was nothing. Nothing. Thieves could've searched the whole house. What would they have found? Nothing.

FLUTE OFFSTAGE: !—!.

(Pause.)

PYOTR NIKOLAYEVICH: And who else could break in at night? There was no one else, right?

VOICE OFFSTAGE: There was no one.

PYOTR NIKOLAYEVICH: There was no one. But once I woke up…

(They take turns standing in front of each other as they speak.)

IVAN IVANOVICH: …and I see an open door, and in the doorway is a woman. I looked directly at her. She looked directly back at me. It was bright. It was morning. I got a good look at her face. I saw her face. And who was she? She was you. *(Points at ELIZAVETA BAM.)* She looked like…

ELIZAVETA BAM: Like me!

IVAN IVANOVICH: I speak therefore I am.

ELIZAVETA BAM: What are you saying?

IVAN IVANOVICH: I speak therefore I am. Soon it will be too late. She listens to me.

(Exit all except ELIZAVETA BAM and IVAN IVANOVICH.)

I asked her why she did it. She said they fought each other with swords. They fought a fair fight, it was not her fault that she killed him. But tell me, why did you kill Pyotr Nikolayevich?

ELIZAVETA BAM: I really didn't kill anyone!

IVAN IVANOVICH: To butcher a man like that. How could you? Really! You did it and I need to know why.

8. TURNING OF THE TABLES

ELIZAVETA BAM: *(Stepping outside of herself.)* Oooooooo-oo-oo-oo-oo

IVAN IVANOVICH: The she-wolf.

ELIZAVETA BAM: Ooooo-oo-oo-oo-oo-oo-oo

IVAN IVANOVICH: Wo-oo-oo-oo-olf.

ELIZAVETA BAM: *(Trembling.)* Oo-oo-oo-oo-ooh prunes.

IVAN IVANOVICH: Gr-rr-rr-reat-grandma mushrooms.

ELIZAVETA BAM: Glory to the highest order!

IVAN IVANOVICH: She's forever ruined. A finger.

ELIZAVETA BAM: A black horse, and on the horse, a soldier.

IVAN IVANOVICH: *(Lighting a match, hands trembling.)* Elizaveta, my dear one.

ELIZAVETA BAM: *(Climbing on her chair.)* My shoulders are the rising sun.

IVAN IVANOVICH: *(Squatting down.)* My legs are cucumbers.

ELIZAVETA BAM: *(Climbing up higher.)* I've said nothing!

IVAN IVANOVICH: *(Lying down.)* Nope, nothing. Nothing. G, g, psh, psh.

ELIZAVETA BAM: *(Raising her arms.)*
Koo-nee-ma-gah-nee-la-va
nee-baooo!

IVAN IVANOVICH: *(On the floor.)*
Here we go round the mulberry bush,
The mulberry bush,
The mulberry bush
Here we go round the mulberry bush
So early in the morning.

ELIZAVETA BAM: *(Yelling.)* Two wicker gates! A shirt! A rope!

IVAN IVANOVICH: *(Lifting himself a little.)* Two carpenters run up and ask: WHAT'S THE MATTER.

ELIZAVETA BAM: Some meat! Varvara Semyona!

IVAN IVANOVICH: *(Yelling through clenched teeth.)* Dancing on the high wire-r-r-r.

ELIZAVETA BAM: *(Jumping off the chair.)* I'm glowing all over-r-r-r!

IVAN IVANOVICH: We don't understand the cubic measurements of this room, good sir.

(The scene changes to a country setting. Enter MOMMY and DADDY.)

ELIZAVETA BAM: *(Running to the other side of the stage.)* It runs in the family. Our people are numbered…

9. A PASTORAL LANDSCAPE

IVAN IVANOVICH: *(Jumping on a chair.)* For the good of the Pennsylvania shepherd and shepher-er-er-er.

ELIZAVETA BAM: *(Jumping on another chair.)* Ivan Iva-a-a-a!

DADDY: *(Holding up a little box.)* This box is made of w-oo-oo-oo!

IVAN IVANOVICH: *(Jumping onto another chair.)* Do show-ow-ow-ow!

DADDY: Have a loo-oo-oo!

MOMMY: Ah-oo-oo-oo-oo.

ELIZAVETA BAM: I found a little mushroo-oo-oo-oo!

IVAN IVANOVICH: Let's go to the lake!

DADDY: Ah-oo-oo-oo-oo.

ELIZAVETA BAM: Ah-oo-oo-oo-oo.

IVAN IVANOVICH: Yesterday I met Johnny!

MOMMY: Seriously-y-y?

IVAN IVANOVICH: Yes, seriously, I met him. I did. I look up and there he is. Johnny. Johnny and his appleseeds. And I said, "You bought those?" And he said, "I bought 'em." And then he up and left.

DADDY: Tell me more plea-ea-ea-ease!

IVAN IVANOVICH: I said, "Did you buy or steal those." And he said, "What do you mean steal them, of course I bought them." And then he left.

MOMMY: Where'd he go-o-o-o-o!

IVAN IVANOVICH: No-o-o-o idea. He just said, "I didn't steal them, I bought them," and went on his way.

10. MONOLOGUE, TANGENT, SOURCE MATERIAL

DADDY: With a less-than-gracious greeting, her sister led her to an open room where gold tables and armchairs were piled up carelessly. Fifteen young maidens happily chanted to themselves, sitting on whatever they could find. All of the maidens were in desperate need of hot iron and they distinguished themselves by rolling their eyes in various ways while chanting.

(Enter THE MAID with a tablecloth and a basket of groceries.)

11. A SPEECH

IVAN IVANOVICH: Friends, we are gathered here today. Hooray!

ELIZAVETA BAM: Hurrah!

MOMMY & DADDY: Huzzah!

IVAN IVANOVICH: *(Trembling and lighting a match.)* I want to tell you that 38 years have passed since I was born.

DADDY & MOMMY: Hip-hip!

IVAN IVANOVICH: Comrades! I have a home. At home is my wife. She has many children. I've counted them—there are ten.

MOMMY: *(Stomping on the ground.)* Darya, Maria, Theodore, Pelagaya, Nina, Alexander, and others, too.

DADDY: All boys?

12. THE CHINAR

ELIZAVETA BAM: *(Running around stage.)*
I've broken free from everything!
I've broken free and run away!
I've broken free and now I'm running!

MOMMY: *(Chasing after ELIZAVETA BAM.)* Do you eat wheat?

ELIZAVETA BAM: Do you eat peas?

DADDY: Do you eat meat? *(Running.)*

MOMMY: Do you eat seeds?

ENTR'ACTE-CATARACT, OR, ACT II

IVAN IVANOVICH: Do you eat beets? *(Starts running.)*

ELIZAVETA BAM: Do you eat sheep?

DADDY: Do you eat beef?

MOMMY: Ouch, my legs are tired.

IVAN IVANOVICH: My liver's tired.

ELIZAVETA BAM: My scissors are tired.

DADDY: My springs are tired.

(Offstage, VOICES sing the overture.)

MOMMY: The balcony door is wide open.

IVAN IVANOVICH: I'll jump to the fourth floor.

ELIZAVETA BAM:
I've broken free and run away!
I've broken free and now I'm running!

(Music is playing.)

DADDY: Officers! My right hand and nose are the same material as my left hand and ear!

(One by one, ALL run offstage.)

CHORUS: *(To the tune of the overture.)*
Bye-bye for now, bye-bye.
!! — !
!! — !
Up above, he says, is a pine
and all around, he says, is darkness.
In the pine, he says, is a bed
and in the bed is someone's lover.
Bye-bye for now, bye-bye.

!! — !
!! — !
Once we ran

in an endless house
and in the highest window
a youngish old man looked through his glasses.
Bye-bye for now, bye-bye.

!! — !
!! — !
The gates opened wide
revealing ! — !.

(The overture plays. The lights go out. A single spotlight falls on PYOTR NIKOLAYEVICH.)

13. THE FOUNDATION

PYOTR NIKOLAYEVICH:
You are broken.
Your chair is broken.

VIOLIN: Pa-Pa-Pi-Pa. Pa-Pa-Pi-Pa.

PYOTR NIKOLAYEVICH:
Stand up to Berlin!
Put on your pelerine!

VIOLIN: Pa-Pa-Pi-Pa. Pa-Pa-Pi-Pa.

PYOTR NIKOLAYEVICH:
Eight minutes
will quietly pass.

(Eight minutes pass.)

VIOLIN: Pa-Pa-Pi-Pa. Pa-Pa-Pi.

PYOTR NIKOLAYEVICH:
You've been given orders
wake up the workers
the platoon or the frontline
to carry the machine gun.

(WAR DRUMS play offstage.)

The pieces were flying
week after week.

SIRENS & DRUMS: Viya-a-boom, boom. Viya-a-boom.

(The lights are getting slowly brighter.)

PYOTR NIKOLAYEVICH:
The bride, she doesn't care,
ignores the Captain's cry.

SIREN: Viya-viya-viya.

PYOTR NIKOLAYEVICH:
Help me, help me right away.
I'm covered in salad and mud.

VIOLIN: Pa-Pa-Pi-Pa. Pa-Pa-Pi-Pa.

(Enter IVAN IVANOVICH.)

14. CLASSICAL INSPIRATION

IVAN IVANOVICH:
Tell me, Pyotr Nikolayevich,
have you been on the faraway mountain?

PYOTR NIKOLAYEVICH:
I have only just returned.
Flowers grow and leaves blow
and there is a cabin, a small wooden house,
and in the house a flame glows
and around the flame the flies hover
and the mosquitoes bang on the window
and a magpie darts back and forth
and a dog barks into the void
and rattles his chains
and the dragonflies reply
mumbling in every language.

IVAN IVANOVICH:
And in this little house, which is small and made of wood, which is called a cabin, wherein a flame glows and glitters, who lives there?

PYOTR NIKOLAYEVICH:
No one lives there.

No one opens the door.
Mice rub flour into their hands.
A lamp glows like rosemary.
A cockroach sits on the stove.

IVAN IVANOVICH:
But who lights the lamp?

PYOTR NIKOLAYEVICH:
No one lights it. It burns by itself.

IVAN IVANOVICH:
Impossible!

PYOTR NIKOLAYEVICH:
Stupid empty words!
Life is unending motion,
we breathe in particles of light,
the planets whir, the earth turns,
day becomes night,
nature intermingles with everything,
beasts swarm in strength and anger,
and humanity conquers the laws
of light and waves.

IVAN IVANOVICH: *(Lighting a match.)*
Oh I get it now, I've got it.
I bow to you and I thank you.
I'm always so interested—
what time is it, do you know?

PYOTR NIKOLAYEVICH:
It's four. Time to eat!
Ivan Ivanovich, let's leave.
But remember, tomorrow eve
Elizaveta Bam will die.

DADDY: *(Entering.)*
The same Elizaveta Bam,
who is my daughter,
whom tomorrow you will murder
and pin to the highest tree
for all the people

and the animals to see?
But I demand
that by the power of my hand
against the laws of the land,
forget Elizaveta Bam.

PYOTR NIKOLAYEVICH:
Try and stop me!
I'll destroy you quickly.
I'll whip your skin
and bruise your limbs
and cut up your body
to blow like ashes in the wind.

IVAN IVANOVICH:
He knows and sees all things,
He is both God and friend to me.
With a single wingbeat
he moves the seas.
With a single swing
of his ax he cuts down mountains and trees.
He lives, he breathes where you cannot see.

DADDY:
Let's fight then, sorcerer,
you with words, I with weapons,
it will only take a minute, or an hour,
or maybe two, or more,
you will die and I will too,
but let my daughter
live a little longer.

15. THE BATTLE OF TWO EPIC HEROES

(Two tables are brought onto the stage.)

IVAN IVANOVICH:
The battle of two epic heroes!
Script—by Emanuel Krisditernik.
Music—by Helios (a Dutch shepherd).
Choreography—by an anonymous traveler.
Church bells will start the fight!

VOICES FROM ACROSS THE ROOM:

The battle of two epic heroes!
Script—by Emanuel Krisditernik.
Music—by Helios (a Dutch shepherd).
Choreography—by an anonymous traveler.
Church bells will start the fight!

(Et cetera. Et cetera.)

BELL: Boom, boom, boom, boom, boom.

PYOTR NIKOLAYEVICH:

Kurabir, daramur
Dinidiri
slakatari pakaradagu,
Da ki chiri, kiri kiri
Zandudila, khabakula
Ge-ll-l
Hanchu ana kudi
Stum chi na lakudi
Para vi na litena
Ge-ll-l
Chapu achapali
Chapaptali mar
Nebelochina
Ge-ll-l

(Raises his hand.)

DADDY:

Let the winged parrot fly
up and into the sun.
Let the sky be gold, wider
when it's over.
Let hooves clatter
through the woods.
Let the wheels of the war wagon
roll freely down the hill.
The knight who sits behind
the table, sword in hand,
lifts his cup and makes a toast
to all the land:

"I raise this cup to the best
of them, Elizaveta Bam
whose hands
are pure and clean
and have touched my chest...
Long live Liz,
one thousand years until death!"

PYOTR NIKOLAYEVICH:
Alright then, let's get started.
Watch closely
how we swing our swords
where the sharp end strikes
and in whose direction.

IVAN IVANOVICH:
Thus I attack on the left!

DADDY: *(Attacking.)*
I swing to the flank, I swing to the right,
every man has a right to fight!
The trees are glowing.
The garden is growing.

PYOTR NIKOLAYEVICH:
Don't lose your mind!
Keep your eye
on the center of the blade,
feel its power to persuade!

DADDY: *(Swinging his sword.)*
Praise the blade—the carborundum!
How it holds the roads together
and glows electric
and defeats our enemies.
Praise the sword! The battle cry!
How it torments the outlaws
and makes men out of children,
and defeats our enemies.
O battle cry! Praise the birds!
How they fly through the air
and cloud the eyes of the infidels

and defeat our enemies.
O praise the birds
and the wisdom of stone!
How it lies still under the pine
and water flows beneath it
to meet our defeated enemies.

PYOTR NIKOLAYEVICH: *(Falling to the ground.)*
I am wounded,
farewell, Elizaveta Bam,
go up to my cabin
on the mountain, and rest there.
And deaf mice will run
all over you
and a hermit cockroach, too.

(Church bells ring.)

You can hear the bells above
the roof ringing ding and dong.
Forgive me, Elizaveta Bam, I was wrong.

IVAN IVANOVICH:
And so the battle of two
epic heroes concludes.

(PYOTR NIKOLAYEVICH is carried offstage.)

16. CHIMES

ELIZAVETA BAM: *(Entering.)*
Ah, Daddy, here you are. I'm very happy.
I was just down at the co-op buying some candy,
I wanted to get a cake to have with tea.

DADDY: *(Unbuttoning his collar.)*
Whew, I'm tired.

ELIZAVETA BAM: What have you been doing?

DADDY: Umm… I was chopping firewood and now I'm exhausted.

ELIZAVETA BAM:
Ivan Ivanovich, run down to the pub

and bring back a bottle of beer and some peas.

IVAN IVANOVICH:
Aha. Peas and half a bottle of beer.
Go to the pub, and from there come here.

ELIZAVETA BAM:
Not a half-bottle, a bottle of beer,
And not to the pub, but to the pea garden!

IVAN IVANOVICH:
I will hide my coat in the pub, instead,
And I will wear half a pea on my head.

ELIZAVETA BAM:
Ah, don't bother with that, just hurry,
Daddy is tired from chopping wood.

DADDY:
Oh, these here women have no ideas,
their minds are the essence of emptiness.

17. PHYSIOLOGICAL INSPIRATION

MOMMY: *(Entering.)* Comrades. That there witch has kilt mah son!

VOICES: Which one?

(Two heads poke out from offstage.)

MOMMY: That one there—the witch with the lips!

ELIZAVETA BAM: Mom, mommy, mother, what are you saying?

(IVAN IVANOVICH lights a match.)

MOMMY: It's your fault that his life ended in a draw.

ELIZAVETA BAM: Can you explain to me what you mean?

MOMMY: *(With a straight face.)* Eek! Eek! Eek!

ELIZAVETA BAM: She's gone crazy!

(DADDY pulls out a handkerchief and begins to dance.)

MOMMY: I'm just a cuttlefish.

(Exit MOMMY and DADDY. The scene shifts back into Elizaveta Bam's apartment.)

ELIZAVETA BAM: They're coming… What have I done!

MOMMY: *(From offstage.)* 3 x 27= 81.

18. REALIST BIT, OFFICIAL AND DRY

(The play more or less begins again.)

ELIZAVETA BAM: Right now. Any minute now. Any second. The door will open and they'll come in… They'll come in. They'll catch me. They'll take me away. Oh god. *(Whispering.)* What have I done! What have I done? If only I had known… Run away! Run? Run where? The door leads to the stairs, they'll find me on the stairs. They're waiting for me on the stairs. They're on the stairs where else could they be! I could go through the window! *(Looks at the window.)* I can't reach it. Can't reach. What should I do? I can't. I hear their footsteps. It's them. I hear them. Their footsteps. I'll lock the door. I won't let them in. Let them knock forever. I won't answer. *(Locks the door.)*

(A firm knock at the door.)

FIRST VOICE: Elizaveta Bam, in the name of the law, I order you to open this door.

(Silence.)

Open the door!

(Silence.)

SECOND VOICE: *(Whispering.)* Let's break down the door.

FIRST VOICE: Elizaveta Bam, let us in or we'll break down the door.

ELIZAVETA BAM: What are you going to do to me?

FIRST VOICE: You're in big trouble.

ELIZAVETA BAM: For what? What have I done?

FIRST VOICE: You are hereby charged with the murder of Pyotr

Nikolayevich Krupernak.

SECOND VOICE: And you'll pay for it.

ELIZAVETA BAM: But I didn't kill anyone!

FIRST VOICE: The court will decide that.

ELIZAVETA BAM: I am at your mercy.

(ELIZAVETA BAM opens the door. PYOTR NIKOLAYEVICH and IVAN IVANOVICH enter dressed as firemen.)

PYOTR NIKOLAYEVICH: You're under arrest.

IVAN IVANOVICH: *(Lighting a match.)* Come with us.

19. THE OPERATIC FINALE

ELIZAVETA BAM: *(Yelling.)* You can lock me up! You can pull out my hair! You can drag me through the gutter! But I didn't kill anyone! I couldn't kill anyone!

PYOTR NIKOLAYEVICH: Calm down, Bam.

IVAN IVANOVICH: Look out into the distance. *(Hiccups.)*

ELIZAVETA BAM: And in the cabin, which is on the mountain, a flame already burns. The mice are wiggling, wiggling their whiskers. And Cockroach Cockroachson sits on the stove. He's wearing a red shirt. He's holding an ax.

PYOTR NIKOLAYEVICH: Elizaveta Bam, hold out your arms, close your eyes, follow me, balance your bones, and keep your tendons under control. Follow me.

(Exit ALL slowly.)

(Curtains.)

December 12-24, 1927.

LAPA

The snore is the end of voices
the snort is a comma
a pillow of knotted hair
crossed with a holy key.
A flower grows from the head
whether a dream or a death
the monster turns through my notebook
the worm swallows night and brearth
rooster feathers fly
on Glinka Platz
a cannon shoots out of a donkey tent
the dream leans against my leg
the west wind—a bucket.
Oh statue of statues
the breath pulses
through the forest's puddles
where wild mushrooms grow in moss
saying to the people: it's nothing
to dive into the well
and cool the marble of your soul.
I am the Landman's bride
but have no strength to roam the country.
I am the weight of a baby.
Be gone tin of the sky!
From now on, I am tin!
And copper and cobalt and spring
into cast iron headfirst
where the blade cries out: knives up!
And the tiger's tail is mossy!
And yet I wander pregnant.
Father in heaven! It's a belt but not me!
Father in heaven! It's a cry but not a mother!
My darling you will be
My darling you will be
My darling you will be

the pines embrace you.
She spoke and fell down.
And the echo cried: Magoga!
Then came the night of John the Baptist
when the grass looked back at God.
Two Nevsky Prospects crisscrossed the forest
a tightrope through the air
the train hissed into
the eyes of heaven's mathematician.
And God spoke: On a smooth stone
stood the landman. He smoked a pipe.
His eyes were sealed with wax.
"I can't see very well," he said.
"Where did my statue go
my light of lights?
A bachelor alone on earth
I hammer my vision into heaven.
By the beating of the heart
time flows by
on the clock and on the table
in the roots and in the trunk.
I'll cross out in my notebook
all my meetings with you statue
for your sake
I'll make my life a slave.
For you I'll rise early
submerge myself in water
legi negi degi vegi
godi bogi nuki vuki."
From Poltava a ghost blew
full of bread and full of flies
who breathe but barely.
Mother buys air for lunch.
I'm the mountain, you're the sand
you're a square, I stand up
I'm a clock, you're a missile
soon the stars will backfire.
Mother will not give us air
thin is the atmosphere
the stars are knives up there.

Mother show me God!
You're a sailboat, I'm a skiff
you're a dog, I'm a judge
you're the pants, I'm the stitch
you're the abyss, I'm the peace
you're the land, I'm the kingdom.

In the name of the Father and the Son and the Holy Spirit.
Amen.

LANDMAN: What is that buzzing?

POWER: That's you sleeping.

LANDMAN: I see a flower above my head. Do I pluck it?

POWER: Pull the Agam down to your feet.

LANDMAN: What's the Agam?

POWER: You don't know?
Once there was an old man. His son worked
in a factory and came home dirty. The old man
boiled water to wash his son's hands.
Cockroaches and pathogens swam
in the water. The son looked through
the water and saw the bottom. In the water swam
the son's reflection. The old man splashed
the reflection out of the water. The reflection
got caught in the pipes and clogged the toilet.
The old man asked the landlord
to fix the toilet. The landlord wrote a referral
and went back to sleep. The next day
the son went to the factory
to make weaponry.

LANDMAN: So what did the old man do?

POWER: You don't know?
The old man was reading a book. He set down
the book, marking his place with a match. He began
to light the stove. He carried firewood

in his crooked arm and thought: my jacket wears
thin where it touches the wood.

LANDMAN: But what is the Agam?

POWER: You don't know?
There are four stars that make a Swan.
This is called the Northern Cross. Recently, among
the stars, a new star appeared—Agam the Swan.
Whoever tears down this star
may choose to be freed from dreaming.

LANDMAN: My arms aren't long enough to reach it.

POWER: Stand up on the roof.

(LANDMAN stands on the roof.)

POWER: How about now?

LANDMAN: Avla dinduri pre pre kru kru.

(A statue on the roof grabs the LANDMAN and makes him light.)

LANDMAN:
I am ligh!
Birds are pocketknives!
Ligh!
Open the lake to make the water ligh!
Open the mountain to let the stream flow ligh.
Stop the clocks because time
has vanished into the land.
Look how ligh I am!

UTYUGOV: *(Looking up through a window.)*
Hey, you up there! Citizen.
I'm trying to read the paper.
And anyway what the hell are you doing up there?
And what's taking you so long?

LANDMAN: *(Laughing.)*
I'm here because of haha and hehe.
Because of ho-ho and heh-heh.
I'm riding into the sky like an eagle

flying like a tear.

UTYUGOV: *(Waving his newspaper around.)*
I'm giving up my living space for a bigger one.
Bap bop baturai! A bigger one!

Remember: koken, foken, zoken, moken!

LANDMAN: Where am I? What is this thing?

KALE ANGEL: The River Nil.

(Wax melts from the LANDMAN'S eyes. The LANDMAN looks at the world around him.)

DESCRIPTION OF THE NIL

It appears as a coffin. Only instead of glaze there is a steamboat and a flying bird. A man lies in the coffin, green with death. To seem alive, he talks all the time:

To make soup you must light the stove and put a pot of water on it. When the water boils throw a carrot into the water… you must put in an arrow and pho… No you must put a carriage in the water. Although that's not exactly true.

Considering what he said, the man was clearly dead. But regardless he held a candlestick in his hand. Essentially, this was the Nil.

Amenhotep sailed the Nil. He wore only underwear and a hat.

DIAGRAM OF AMENHOTEP

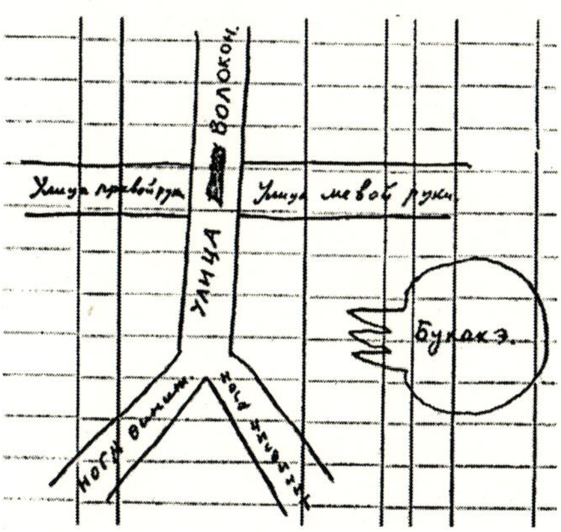

Meanwhile, a certain Nikolai Ivanovich looked under the tail of an ibis to see what was there.

LANDMAN: Nikolai Ivanovich, what did you find?

NIKOLAI IVANOVICH: Well, you see, I still haven't figured it out. The feathers are getting in the way.

LANDMAN: Seeing is hard to do.

NIKOLAI IVANOVICH: It was better back there. Back there, you could get buckwheat porridge with butter, or even better, if it's cold with milk, and you eat it.

LANDMAN: Or cheesecake. Especially if you eat it the easy way, with your hands.

NIKOLAI IVANOVICH: *(Singing.)* Or soup. Did you know, to make soup you boil meat and fish in water.

(THE DECEASED sit down with them.)

THE DECEASED: Er put a tooth in the sooоup. Er asparaguses. Er a kid's buk. Er drydnut.

(SOMEONE screams beyond the horizon.)

... A smaller one for a bigger one. Bap bop baturai!

Amenhotep rises out of the water and walks across the sharp rocks. It's painful to walk and Amenhotep flails around and sits down now and then. Now he reaches the sand and then he runs freely and falls to the ground and rolls around.

"I'll have a smoke," says Amenhotep. Everyone is silent. Nikolai Ivanovich looks angrily under the ibis's tail.

Amenhotep takes off his underwear, wrings them out and hangs them in the sun to dry. He looks around to see whether a woman is coming. There're no women, but on the shore of the candlestick, he sees a female marble statue.

LANDMAN: Well guys, I've caught my breath now, and it's time to get going.

Where to? asks Nikolai Ivanovich.

To the Swans, says the Landman.

And the Landman rises up higher.

Here are two trees in love with each other.

One tree is a wolf and the other is a she-wolf.

When the Landman looked at them from around the corner, the wolf ran to the border.

The Landman hid himself.

The wolf kissed the she-wolf.

The Landman came out from his hiding place.

Where is the swan? he asked the wolves.

Then came the watchman in a white coat. He held a long scraper.

The Swans, he said, sniffing a fistful of bread so as not to cry.

They're over there. Look in that house.

The Landman walked along the pond. The pond was covered in snow.

Birdhouse

The birdhouse reeked. A little girl ate rice cakes in the corner. She was filthy and wild. There were giant potholes in the asphalt floor and puddles filled them. An old man wearing a long black overcoat walked through the puddles and looked crooked at the birds. The room was divided by a knee-high partition. Large birds walked back and forth behind the partition. The pelicans sat by the puddles and bathed themselves in the dirty water. The little girl set down her rice cake and began to sing. Her mouth was a perfect round circle.

THE LITTLE GIRL SANG:

Plea plea
Klya klya
Smakh smakh gapchanuk
vekibaki sabache

dubti kept aldalab
smerkh purk birds
sali or eh or ah
soo suo sya se
soulvei vie vi
vie vao vua vi
vua vya vao viu
tweet tweet tweet tweet
zakurak.

The oldest pelican began to dance. A gray comb stuck out of his head. His eyes were red. They pierced the sea shell. First, he marched in place for a long time. Then he began moving forward and backward, keeping his head fixed at a point in space. Only his neck was bent. Then the pelican dropped a wing to the floor and spun around on one leg, stomping with the other. He danced over here and over there. He swam like an aristocrat, dragging both wings across the floor.

The rest of the birds kept quiet, moving out of the way and putting their noses against the wall so as not to watch the pelican's dance. Shut up! yelled the old man in the long black overcoat. But no one listened.

The little girl kept singing. The pelican kept dancing.

And this is the sky?! said the old man. Yuck yuck yuck! How disgusting!

Why do you think this is the sky? asked another such old man, appearing out of nowhere, to the first old man.

Oh never mind, said the first old man. My entire life I refused to sing stupid songs. All these songs are all ugly.

Why don't you just try to sing for yourself, said the same such old man.

But the first old man shook his head, which caused his glasses to fall from his nose and into a puddle.

Now do you see? Do you!? said the angry old man.

The door opened and the Landman walked into the bird house.

Have you seen the Swan? he yelled.

I'm over here! the Swan yelled back.

Wow! Is this the sky? asked the Landman.

This is the sky! yelled the sky.

Just then the Angel Kale flew by and once again the Landman entered the birdhouse.

Have you seen the Swan? he yelled.

I'm over here! the Swan yelled back.

Wow! This is the sky! yelled the Landman.

Yes, this is the sky, said the Angel Kale.

This is heaven
where the Swan is sovereign
quickly, daughter,
go and bring us water.

The little girl went to retrieve some water. Angel Kale drank the water, wiped his mustache, and said: "The bastard's cold, but delicious. Now look: a typhoid fever rules over us, but it doesn't matter. All you need to do is rub your belly once in the morning and once at night while saying: grumble, grumble, but don't get sick."

Suddenly, with one giant leap the Landman jumped over the partition, grabbed the Swan, and fell into the earth.

Where he fell, a pine tree grew with arms and a hat and she was named Maria Ivanovna.

The Conversation Between Angel Dale And Maria Ivanovna

ANG. DALE: Astonishing! And I'm just wondering here, do you have a ticket?

MAR. IV.: Ha ha ha, what nonsense! After all, I am a turkey.

ANG. DALE: Don't talk to me like that. After all, I am an angel.

MAR. IV.: Why?

ANG. DALE: Because I have wings.

MAR. IV.: Ha ha ho! But, after all, these birds also have wings!

ANG. DAEL: You think like Professor Permyakov. He and the security guard Fadey put me in this chicken coop.

(MARIA IVANOVNA yawns and falls asleep. ANGEL DABBAGE wakes her.)

ANGEL DEIL: Maria Ivanovna wake up. I'll tell you my idea about axles.

MARIA IVANOVNA STILL IN HER DREAM: Darling, dearest, dear. Don't ask me that question. I want to live.

ANGEL DEIL: No seriously, Maria Ivanovna, I really love wheat. Do you know, it even grows in manure. Manure! Can you believe it!

MAR. IV. THE PINE TREE: You're kidding! Fi Donc! Manzure and swheat porridge!

ANGEL DEVIL: It's the truth, Madam Maria Ivanovna. Although, of course, it depends on what kind of manure. Horse is the best. There's not too much of that you-know-what, and just enough of the straw-type stuff. Cow poop works OK, too. Although, you know, it's a bit sticky. And the dog's? Bleh! It's just plain shit! There's no wheat in it. But I eat it. I eat it anyway. I do. But, as I was saying...

MARIA IVANOVNA: *(Covering her ears.)* Truly, an angel! He'll eat anything! Who knows, maybe you eat vomit, too.

How can I explain what happened next? Well, the Angel Devil rushed in, but Maria Ivanovna started screaming and swearing which caused the Angel Devil to cover his mouth so fast that he became dizzy and fell to the earth.

Now Andrei straws drynvaku and spitting the gusmakrel or the feces of freedom and the kulpa facanath shtos palmadeub.

glAvNabor

Mak	———	leyapiye
mamak		leyapiye gae
mamamak		leyapiye gae oo

V. ——— The kite gnawed the bone.
Kh. The Landman fell into the earth.

moi
voi
koi
vedi
dui
bui
vehe
aye
hiye
seo
puye
plyaye
klyoe
poko
pliye
plyoe
qliuye
moye
foye
toye
nyunya
tyupya
kyoyo
pyoyo
qyuyu
yuyu
plyao
klyao
klyas
klya pa feo
pelsipao
guldegreya

pyan
koken, foken, zoken, moken

HOW THE LANDMAN RETURNED TO EARTH

UTYUGOV: *(Waving a portable stove.)*
Bap bop baturai!
Dinner went well.
I ate a plate of soup
with dill, with onions, with an arrow.
And vinaigrette potatoes with horseradish,
all darling Tanya's handiwork,
ate until I was full. And hurried
out the door, as is my hidden nature.
When food boils as a spring
in the bomb coffin stomach
blood runs through the veins
that stitch the body's fabric
the cheek burns red
in the pulse pao puo po
pendi pyundi as it goes
pounding the eardrum po po po
while I hear the buzz
from heaven through my window
the rattling wind
the world long ago birthed.
It's too cramped to live.
Abandon cage!
Fly to the sky!

(Waves his portable stove.)

The sky skybo skybodi
bubi the sky ne skybo
Who is flying from here?
nebanbanba skyobei!
Come here skybo, razbebo

VLADIMIR KHLEBNIKOV: *(Riding in on a horse.)* pulsh pelsh pepopei!

UTYUGOV:

What, Horseman?
What's with the riding?
What do you see?
What are you? What are you
saying, dear horseman?
I have not seen the hills in so long,
pine trees, pastures, and grasses
can you look at nature
with your own eyes, horseman?
I am a modern citizen
I cannot know the stones
shrubs, trebs, trunks, moshes, trees,
I only know hee hee and hee.

KHLEBNIKOV: *(Riding on a bull.)* But do you know the sky, Utyugov?

UTYUGOV:

I know the sky—the sky is tin.
In the tin parts—the parts are ten.

KHLEBNIKOV: *(Riding on a cow.)*

That's not the sky.
That's just a hand
the universal man and his little fire.

UTYUGOV:

O! I'm tired of the sky.
It hangs over our heads
leaking if rain
knocks from above.
If someone walks in heaven
it fills with thunder
and the brick walls quiver
and clocks strike out
and down pours
the grandfather of foam
heavenly water's waterfall.
Once the wind
carried away the sky
like straw the poor people cried

and the bulls bitterly wept.
When a shepherd looked into heaven
to find the constellation of the Goat
he thought he saw fish
swallowing the air.
Depth and the dove became one.
The brain's boat and memory's rudder
carried the constellation of the Swan.
The loud flowers grew
and the dark trees blew.
The shepherd fell deep in thought.
"Of course," he thought, "I'm right
something is happening.
Why has the earth become cold?
I'm losing my breath
I'm indifferent to everything."
Thus he spake and lay on the grass.
"Now I understand.
The sky is gone.
O sky sky, now empty
now mere color
sky blue like a flower
as long as cattails
as fast as skis.
Humanity! breathe!
We're suffocating, but we will
find you fugitive
you cannot hide!"
Thus he spake.
And then he lay
in the ditch, folding his psalms to pray.

KHLEBNIKOV: *(Riding on a sheet of paper.)* And what did the sky return?

UTYUGOV:

Yes, that I did.
I climbed a tower
took a rope
held a candle
set fire to the village

opened the floodgate
drank up the ocean
wound up the clock
broke the chair
and the sky fell through the ether
and returned to its stall.

KHLEBNIKOV: *(Galloping in an aqueduct.)*
Do you remember: the day drank itself.
And did you know: the wind was I!

UTYUGOV: *(Waving his portable stove.)*
Bap bop baturai!
Stop that horseman!
Stop him or he'll tear down the sky!
Koken, foken, zoken, moken!

Out of thin air the Landman flies, carrying the Swan in his arms. The Landman approaches the roofs. On one such roof is a statue of a woman. She grabs the Landman and he becomes heavy. The Landman looks into heaven, where he had been.

LANDMAN: Look at where I've been!

UTYUGOV: *(Looking through a window.)* Did you happen to see a horseman on your way?

LANDMAN: What did he look like?

UTYUGOV: Oh you know, like this, with this or that kind of face.

LANDMAN: He rode on a pencil?

UTYUGOV: Yes yes yes—that's him! Ugh, why did you let him go? He'll go directly to the K.G.B. He… I can't say anything else. Or, no, I must say it… I need to say it… He, that horseman… he might tear down the sky.

LANDMAN: The sky? Ha ha ha! i! e! m. m. m. Fo fo fo! gi gi gi! Tear down the sky! What? Tear down the sky? Fo fo fo! Impossible! The sky gee gee gee you can't tear it down! A security guard watches the sky around the clock. Look that's him! The lightning rod. The guard will break anyone who dares to touch the sky. Do you understand?

UTYUGOV: And what is that you're holding?

LANDMAN: Oh this? This is just a little chickadee. I caught it up in heaven.

UTYUGOV:

Hold on, wait a second.
That's a piece of the sky!
Guard! Bap bop baturai!
Let's get him, boys!

Nikolai Ivanovich and Amenhotep began to run, heeding the call. The ibis was relieved now that no one was examining his nether parts—and he rejoiced in the feeling of freedom. Nikolai Ivanovich quickly ran. The ibis squinted and drank the air.

"What's happening? Where? Why?" yelled Nikolai Ivanovich.

"Over here," yelled Utyugov, "this citizen tore down a piece of the sky and now he's calling it a bird."

"Where berd? What's berd?" Nikolai Ivanovich bustled. "Here's a bird," he yelled and shoved the ibis into Utyugov's face.

Meanwhile, the Landman stood by the wall, clinging to the Swan and looking around for a place to hide.

"Allow me," said Amenhotep. "I'll take care of this. Where's the thief? What kind of times are we living in! Eh? All you ever hear about is scandal, understocked supermarkets, and a lack of cigarettes. You know, I myself went over to Lakhta river and saw for myself. The summer renters just sit there in the forest and frankly it's embarrassing what's going on. It's a debauchery."

"Koken foken zoken moken!" Utyugov would not stop. "What are we going to do to this thief? Let's glue him to the wall. Does anyone have glue?"

"Don't waste your time," said a seasonal worker, appearing from nowhere, drinking cologne as he passed. "We need to beat people like him."

"Beat him! Beat! Bap bop baturai!" yelled Utyugov.

(AMENHOTEP and NIKOLAI IVANOVICH surround the LANDMAN.)

POWER:

Crash proh manhaleet.
Pull the Agam down to your feet

(Pause.)

Briefly all is calm. The light stops. Everyone who slept wakes up. Even Podkhelukov, the Soviet official, wakes up. *(He has a neat beard without a mustache.)* Podkhelukov looks out the window. On the street, a salesman of kerosene blows into his trumpet.

PODKHELUKOV: It's impossible to sleep. There's a bedbug infestation. Look at how they've eaten at my body.

PODKHELUKOV'S WIFE: *(Quickly counting the teeth in her mouth, speaks with a whistle.)* I am uiki-si-li-ao.

PODKHELUKOV: Why are you in such a good mood?

PODKHELUKOV'S WIFE: *(Hugging AMENHOTEP.)* My lover is here!

PODKHELUKOV: Ugh, disgusting! He's only wearing underwear. *(Thinking.)* And he's all sweaty, too.

(Trembling, AMENHOTEP looks at PODKHELUKOV and covers his nakedness with his hands.)

POWER:

Fee a fara. Fo.

(He takes the LANDMAN by the hand and runs toward an iceberg.)

An iceberg, an iceberg is the sea frozen
into the shape of an apron.

KaKhavaKha

Power says: msan klik didubei

Landman sings: I see a dream

Power says: ganglau geh

Landman sings: the dream is a flower

Power says: pckimi wleruf

Landman sings: now I am asleep

Power says: pull the Agam down to your feet

Landman babbles: Lily bai

Rabinovich—who hides under beds, who doesn't wash his feet, who has raped other men's wives—opens the basket and puts a baby inside. The baby falls asleep right away and a flower grows from its head.

KaKhavaKha

Again our eyes are sealed and waxy.
Again we dream about the great galaxy.

June 24-August 17, 1930, Petersburg.

THE STORY OF ZDYGR APPR

ANDREI SEMYONOVICH: Hello, Petya.

PYOTR PAVLOVICH: Hello, hello. Guten Morgen. Where going?

Andrei Semyonovich stretched out his hand to Pyotr Pavlovich and Pyotr Pavlovich grabbed Andrei Semyonovich's hand and shook it so vigorously that they ripped off Andrei Semyonovich's arm and Andrei Semyonovich ran off in horror. Pyotr Pavlovich ran after Andrei Semyonovich yelling: "I ripped off your arm, you pig, and, just you wait, when I catch you, I'll rip off your head, too!"

Andrei Semyonovich leapt suddenly and cleared a ditch but Pyotr Pavlovich wasn't able to cross the ditch and were left on this side of it.

ANDREI SEMYONOVICH: What? Couldn't catch up?

PYOTR PAVLOVICH: Didya see this? *(He holds up ANDREI SEMYONOVICH'S arm.)*

ANDREI SEMYONOVICH: That's my arm!

PYOTR PAVLOVICH: Yes, it's your arm! Now what'll you wave with?

ANDREI SEMYONOVICH: A tissue.

PYOTR PAVLOVICH: Not bad, not bad. Well then, there's nothing else to say. But put one hand in your pocket, and you won't be able to scratch your head.

ANDREI SEMYONOVICH: Petya! Look: I'll give you something for it—just hand over my arm.

PYOTR PAVLOVICH: No, I won't hand it over. Don't even bother asking. If you'd like, we can go see Professor Tartarelin, he'll fix it.

(ANDREI SEMYONOVICH jumped with joy and went to see PROFESSOR TARTARELIN.)

ANDREI SEMYONOVICH: Most esteemed Professor, please fix my right arm. My acquaintance Pyotr Pavlovich ripped it off and won't give it back to me.

Pyotr Pavlovich were standing in the professor's foyer, doubled over with demonic laughter. Tucked disdainfully in their armpit like a briefcase was Andrei Semyonovich's arm.

After examining Andrei Semyonovich's shoulder, the professor lit his pipe-cigarette and pronounced, "It's a large shrape."

ANDREI SEMYONOVICH: Excuse me?

PROFESSOR: A large shrape.

ANDREI SEMYONOVICH: Scrape?

PROFESSOR: Yes, yes, yes. Shrake. Shoo-rapke!

ANDREI SEMYONOVICH: A scrape where the whole arm's missing…

(Laughter emanates from the foyer.)

PROFESSOR: Oh! Whuch that shound?

ANDREI SEMYONOVICH: It's nothing. Just ignore it.

PROFESSOR: Ho! Whish pleashure. May I read you a little something?

ANDREI SEMYONOVICH: Um… you'll fix my arm?

PROFESSOR: Yes, yes, yes, but later. Let's read a bit first. Sit down.

(Both sit.)

PROFESSOR: Would you like me to read you my science?

ANDREI SEMYONOVICH: Please! Sounds very interesting.

PROFESSOR: Only I've written it in verse.

ANDREI SEMYONOVICH: Sounds extremely interesting!

PROFESSOR: I'll read from here to there, hah. This here's about internal organs, and there's about joints.

PYOTR PAVLOVICH: *(Walking into the room.)*
Zdygr appr oostr oostr
I'm handling someone else's arm
zdygr appr oostr oostr

where's Professor Tartarelin?
zdygr appr oostr oostr
where's the office clock?
if these ticking whatsits
with broken gears and weights
the only lady's tiny watches
clocked parabolas in flight
zdygr appr oostr oostr
fucked up the motion of the clock
in its place—the karabistr
on a placemat zdygr appr
with an arm, bottomless as rocks
oriented like arrows
from tick to tock
flying as if on fire
below the clock's white face
a blinchik winds up oostr oostr
swaddled in a robe of lace
sits the karabistr
he monitors seconds
with an engine regulated
so time won't walk away
where Professor Tartarelin
where Andrei Semyonich zdygr
the one-armed zdygr appr
fixes zdygr appr oostr
reattaches arm to shoulder
nails on each finger
zdygr appr hammers
zdygr appr oostr thumps

PROFESSOR: Was it you who maimed this citizen, Pyotr Pavlovich?

PYOTR PAVLOVICH: I tore his arm off at the seam.

ANDREI SEMYONOVICH: And he ran after me.

PROFESSOR: Answer me!

(PYOTR PAVLOVICH laughs.)

KARABISTR: Gvindaleya!

PYOTR PAVLOVICH: Karabistr!

KARABISTR: Gvindalan!

PROFESSOR: Tell me how it happened.

ANDREI SEMYONOVICH:
I was recently out walking
when who do I see but Petya
calmly walking toward me—
only as if he hadn't seen me
and wanted to sneak by me.
I called out to him: Ah, Petya!
Hello, Petya, my compadre,
it seems you didn't see
that I am walking toward ya.

PYOTR PAVLOVICH:
But the rule of circumstance
and the intersection of events
since the dawn of time
governs us like children,
starves us into a hunger-trance,
and whips us penitent.

PROFESSOR: Well, well, so it is, of course. A confluence of circumstance. That's right. A law.

Just then Pyotr Pavlovich leaned toward the professor and bit off his ear. While Andrei Semyonovich ran off to get a policeman, Pyotr Pavlovich threw Andrei Semyonovich's arm on the ground, placed Professor Tartarelin's bitten-off ear on the table, and fled down the back staircase unseen.

Professor Tartarelin lay on the ground and moaned.

"Oh-oh-oh, it hurts!" moaned the professor. "It burns and bleeds! Where can I find a Good Samaritan, who will flush and disinfect my scrape?!"

It was a lovely evening. The stars, situated in the sky according to fixed patterns, shone down from above. Andrei Semyonovich, breathing with his whole chest, began to drag two policemen to Professor Tartarelin's. Waving his only arm, Andrei Semyonovich recounted what happened while they walked.

One of the cops asked Andrei Semyonovich:

"And who's the crook that did this?"

Andrei Semyonovich didn't tattle on his friend. He wouldn't even say his name. Then both cops asked Andrei Semyonovich:

"So, have you known him long?"

"Since I was child," said Andrei Semyonovich.

"And what does he look like?" asked the cops.

"His distinguishing feature is a long, black beard," said Andrei Semyonovich.

The cops stopped speaking, pulled their belts a little tighter and, opening their mouths very wide, began to sing in sonorous, nocturnal voices:

Ah, how interesting—
he was a young man,
and when he grew up,
he grew a beard.

"Your voices aren't half bad. Please allow me to express my deepest gratitude," said Andrei Semyonovich and, because he had no arm, extended his empty sleeve to the cops.

"We can also lecture briefly on scientific processes," the cops said in unison.

Andrei Semyonovich waved his empty sleeve.

"The earth has seven oceans," began the cops. "The scientific physicists studying sunspots have come to the conclusion that there's no hydrogen on other planets, and so any kind of cohabitation there would be unseemly.

"In our atmosphere, there is a point, which will fix every center.

"The English crematorium Albert Einstein invented a scheme according to which all kinds of things are relative."

"Oh, sweet police!" Andrei Semyonovich entreated. "Let's get there before that young man with a beard kills Professor Tartarelin."

One cop was named Volodya, and the other, Seryozha. Volodya grabbed Seryozha by the hand, and Seryozha grabbed Andrei Semyonovich by the sleeve, and all three began to run.

"Look, three schoolgirls running!" the carriage drivers yelled as they ran by. One even whipped Seryozha on the ass.

"Hey, you! I'll fine you for that on my way back!" cried Seryozha, not letting go of Andrei Semyonovich's sleeve.

When they reached the professor's house, all three said "Tprrr!" and stopped.

"Up the stairs, to the third floor!" ordered Andrei Semyonovich.

"Hoch!" the cops cried and rushed up the stairs.

They knocked down the door with their shoulders and flew into Professor Tartarelin's office. Professor Tartarelin was sitting on the floor. His wife was kneeling before him, sewing his ear back on with pink silk thread. The professor held scissors in his hands. He was cutting a hole in the center of his wife's dress. When his wife's naked stomach appeared, the professor rubbed it with his palm and looked into it as if into a mirror.

"Watch where you're sewing! Can't you see that one ear's higher than the other?" the professor said, annoyed.

His wife ripped off the ear and began to sew it on again.

The woman's naked tummy overjoyed the professor. His whiskers bristled and his eyes began to dance.

"Katenka," said the professor, "why not sew my ear somewhere else, maybe it'd be better on my cheek."

Katenka, the wife of Professor Tartarelin, patiently ripped off the ear for the second time and began sewing it to the professor's cheek.

"Oh, how it tickles! Ha ha ha! How it tickles!" the professor laughed, but, seeing the cops standing on the threshold, he shut up and put on a serious face.

OFFICER SERYOZHA: Where's the victim?

OFFICER VOLODYA: Who here had an ear bitten off?

PROFESSOR: *(Rising to his feet.)* Gentlemen! I am a man who has studied science already for 56 years, thank god, and I never meddle in anyone else's affairs. If you think my ear's been bitten off, then you are sorely mistaken. As you can see, I have two undamaged ears. One, it's true, on my cheek, but such was my wish.

OFFICER SERYOZHA: Indeed, it's true, he has two undamaged ears.

OFFICER VOLODYA: My cousin has eyebrows growing under his nose.

OFFICER SERYOZHA: Not eyebrows, but whiskers.

KARABISTR: Fasfalakat!

PROFESSOR: Visiting hours are over.

PROFESSOR'S WIFE: It's time for bed.

ANDREI SEMYONOVICH: *(Leaving.)* It's 11:30.

OFFICERS IN UNISON: Goodnight.

ECHO: Sleep well.

(The PROFESSOR lies down on the floor. The rest also lie down and go to sleep.)

The Dream

quietly the ocean splashes
the gray rocks duh-dun
quietly the ocean flashes
a person sings in the duh-dun
quietly across the sea
zoom white elephants of fear
slippery fish croon
stars fall from the moon
a shoddy little cabin stands
its doors open wide as hands
its warm oven entices
in the house a guard dozes
a babushka sleeps on the roof here
her nose is askew
quietly the wind splashes an ear
blows hair askew
in the tree a cuckoo
looks through his glasses to the north
don't look my cuckoo
don't look all night to the north
there, only the wind karabistr
keeps time in numbers and days
only the hawk zdygr oostr
lies in wait for his prey

PYOTR PAVLOVICH:
Someone fell asleep on the dark stair,
I grope and sniff: table and chair,
I bump into a settee,
I see a bergamot tree,

I hurry, I pick a pear—
what the fuck! It's an ear!
I'm afraid, I run to the right,
an oak grove grew in overnight,
I turn back this way and that,
I bump into an aristocrat,
my legs bend, stretch out to lie down,
I thought: the doors are an oven,
jumped left – there's a bed,
help me!…

PROFESSOR: *(Waking up.)* Helr?…

ANDREI SEMYONOVICH: *(Jumping to his feet.)* Oof! Quite a dream—it was as if all our ears had been ripped off.

(He turns on the light.)

It turns out, while everyone was sleeping, Pyotr Pavlovich walked around and ripped off everyone's ears.

Seryozha the cop remarks: "A dream come true!"

March-April 1929.

SECTION II: SHORTER PLAYS IN PROSE

UNTITLED (ELENA IVANOVNA)

ELENA IVANOVNA: Well, Fadei Ivanovich, all rain falls.

DADDY: Yes, be quiet, Elena Ivanovna, the meadows are dying.

ELENA IVANOVNA: It's good we're sitting under a roof, but what if someone were out in the field? Hm?

DADDY: It's bad for a traveler to be without a house.

ELENA IVANOVNA: Would you like some more tea?

DADDY: Splash another skull.

(Silence. DADDY drinks a little tea and dozes off.)

ELENA IVANOVNA: And Olga isn't writing anything.

(DADDY mutters unintelligibly.)

ELENA IVANOVNA: Isn't writing and isn't writing.

DADDY: How isn't she writing?

ELENA IVANOVNA: I said Olga isn't writing.

DADDY: That is, what Olga?

ELENA IVANOVNA: Yes, Olga! What's with you! You don't know Olga?

DADDY: Ah… Olga? Well, and what is she?

ELENA IVANOVNA: Yes, well, I said she isn't writing.

DADDY: Ayayay.

RACHTANOV: *(Entering.)* And Sergei proposed to Olga. *(Exits.)*

ELENA IVANOVNA: Sergei, look at him! And she? *(To DADDY.)* Did you hear?

DADDY: What?

ELENA IVANOVNA: The proposal?

DADDY: Well and he?

ELENA IVANOVNA: No, Olga.

DADDY: Isn't writing what?

ELENA IVANOVNA: To get married.

DADDY: Ayayay.

ELENA IVANOVNA: What a mess.

RACHTANOV: *(Entering.)* Kolya crushed the metal sofa. There.

ELENA IVANOVNA: Wait wait, what's this?

DADDY: *(Quickly.)* Horrible, horrible! What a catastrophe! They crushed the metal sofa…

ELENA IVANOVNA: You entrust the metal sofa to him, and immediately he tries to crush it.

RACHTANOV: *(Crosses the stage and claps before and after saying the following.)* And on Tuesday Kolya ate his home.

ELENA IVANOVNA: So it goes. He—

May 1929.

UNTITLED (A NAME FOR OURSELVES)

TETERNIK: *(Running on stage.)* Hello! Hello! Hello! Hello!

KAMUSHKOV: You're late. We've been waiting for you.

THE GREEK: Yeah yeah yeah. We've been waiting!

LAMPOV: Well. *(Pause.)* Explain yourself!

TETERNIK: *(Looking at his watch.)* Am I really late? Well… Okay, yeah, I'm late… Okay!

KAMUSHKOV: Okay. Let's continue.

THE GREEK: Let's continue!

(EVERYONE sits down in their place and grows silent.)

(Minutes pass.)

KAMUSHKOV: How many times do I have to tell you people, we need to come up with a name for ourselves.

THE GREEK & LAMPOV: Hear! Hear!

KAMUSHKOV: *(Mockingly.)* Hear! Hear!… We need to come up with a name!… You, Greek!

(THE GREEK stands up.)

What name have you come up with?

THE GREEK: Nypyrsytet.

KAMUSHKOV: No. No. No good. Just think for a minute, I mean seriously, ask yourself: "Why did I choose this name?" Think about it, it sounds bad and it means nothing… It's stupid… And yet, there must have been some reason you chose it… So, let's hear it! Tell us, why did you suggest such a stupid name?

THE GREEK: It's stupid.

KAMUSHKOV: You understand, don't you?… Sit down, please… People, come on, we need a name for what we are!…

(LAMPOV stands up.)

What've you got?

LAMPOV: I suggest, "The Folk Dancers." Or, "Jelly," or… "My Sicilian"… What? You don't like them?… Ok, then, what about "The Pinnacle," or "Sugar Daddies," or "Mortar and Candle,"… or…

KAMUSHKOV: *(Shaking his fist.)* Idiot! Jackass!

December 26, 1929.

THE BARONESS AND THE INKSTAND

BOBROV: *(Pointing to CHRISTOPHER COLUMBUS.)* Christopher Columbus.

CHRISTOPHER COLUMBUS: *(Pointing to BOBROV.)* Bobrov.

BOBROV: If you're interested in my upbringing, I'll tell you about it. I'll tell you.

CHRISTOPHER COLUMBUS: Yes, yes, please tell me.

BOBROV: As they say: what's there to hide?

CHRISTOPHER COLUMBUS: Very, very interesting!

BOBROV: Well, I'll say this: what was my upbringing like? Institutional.

CHRISTOPHER COLUMBUS: Ah, go on, go on, please.

BOBROV: My father put me in an orphanage. And.

(He keeps his mouth open. CHRISTOPHER stands on his toes and peers into Bobrov's mouth.)

But then again, I am a merchant.

(CHRISTOPHER jumps back.)

CHRISTOPHER COLUMBUS: I- I- was only curious to see what you had there… uh… uh…

BOBROV: Now. So, in the orphanage, I fell in love with a baroness and her inkstand.

CHRISTOPHER COLUMBUS: You really fell in love?

BOBROV: Don't be a pain. Yes, in love!

CHRISTOPHER COLUMBUS: A miracle.

BOBROV: Don't be a pain. Yes, a miracle!

CHRISTOPHER COLUMBUS: Fascinating.

BOBROV: Don't be a pain. Yes, fascinating.

CHRISTOPHER COLUMBUS: Tell me, please!

BOBROV: If you, Christopher Columbus, say anything more…

(The scene changes quickly. BOBROV is sitting and eating soup. His WIFE enters wearing a single shirt and carrying an umbrella.)

BOBROV: Where're you going?

WIFE: There.

BOBROV: Where's there?

WIFE: Just over there.

BOBROV: There or there?

WIFE: No, not there, but there.

BOBROV: What?

WIFE: What "what"?

BOBROV: Where're you going?

WIFE: I fell in love with the Baroness and her Inkstand.

BOBROV: That's nice.

WIFE: That's nice, but Christopher Columbus shoved his bike into our cook.

BOBROV: Poor cook.

WIFE: The poor thing is sitting in the kitchen, writing a letter to her village, and the bike's just sticking out…

BOBROV: Yes, yes. That's the case. I remember, the same happened at the orphanage in 1887. We had a teacher. We rubbed his face with turpentine and stuck him under the kitchen table.

WIFE: My god, why're you telling me this?

BOBROV: That's still the case.

(THE SAUSAGE MAN exits.)

November 11-30, 1930.

UNTITLED (THE GUESTS)

There's a tall person deftly playing the harmonica
There are four people behind him listening quietly
Again there's the musician whose fingers move lightly
Again there are four people behind him, quiet as the grave
He must be a sorcerer, playing everything exactly the same
He walks along the road to the park, behind him the four follow
I'll sit on the bench not more than a month
You'll sit on the bench till Easter
He'll sit on the bench through four holidays
We'll sit on the bench near the river
You'll sit on the bench near the river
They sit as you can see they are resting
Above them flutter butterflies
Above them flit mosquitos
Made of wood

(The GUESTS move in.)

FOURTH GUEST:
The porridge is served.

GUEST WITH A FAN:
Which of us will kiss the hostess or the host?

FLEA-RIDDEN GUEST:
Oh shit! My top's sleeveless!

TATIANA NIKOLAYEVICH:
He-he, this morning I was talking with flour in my mouth and nearly choked.

UNCLE VOLL:
Oh dear, my youth is gone!

HOST:
Gather round the table, guests.
There is cake and boiled eggs.
Here's the salt and here's the flu.
Here are nails. I'm through.

GUESTS: We don't want food, we want to dance!

HOSTESS: Musicians! Yes! two!… three!

(The MUSICIANS jump into the water.)

Well, that didn't work out as planned.

FLEA-RIDDEN GUEST: Should we go for a swim or what?

EIGHT-GUEST CHOIR: Well, indeed, that too!

PRINCESS MANKA-DUNKA: Gentlemen, I'm all freckled, you see, but it would be lovely… I swear!

GUEST FYODOR: He-he, with pleasure.

SOLDIER IN PANTIES: Princess Manka-Dunka, please allow me to bring you a bouquet of flowers.

GUEST FYODOR: Or take this comb.

SOLDIER IN PANTIES: Or take this speck of dust.

GUESTS: Quiet, quiet! Listen! Now Uncle Voll will tell us a story.

UNCLE VOLL: *(Sitting on a chair.)* I've read a good story in a certain French book. Should I tell it?

GUESTS: Yes, yes!

TATIANA NIKOLAYEVICH: Absolutely!

UNCLE VOLL: Once, a young girl brought her poor mother a pie filled with cabbage and onion. The pie was baked in clarified butter and sprinkled with cumin.

GUESTS: Ha ha ha ha ha! We're dying!

UNCLE VOLL: Wait, that's not all, there's still more! A kind gentleman gives the girl a gold coin and says: Here's a gold coin, girl, bring it to your poor mother.

GUESTS: Ha ha ha! Cleverly done!

UNCLE VOLL: And she thinks for a while then says: I'm a laundress.

GUESTS: Ha ha ha!

UNCLE VOLL: Then the kind gentleman pulls a grand piano from his pocket.

GUESTS: Ha ha ha ha!

PRINCESS MANKA-DUNKA: Oh, I can't take it! Even my teeth hurt! I swear!

HOST: Well, time to go home.

HOSTESS: Goodbye, goodbye dear guests!

GUESTS: Goodbye, goodbye. We'll go and set our homes on fire!

HOSTESS: *(Blushing)* Honestly, you flatter me!

HOST: Come again!

1931.

A CONTROVERSY

(A PUPPET and an ALMSGIVER sitting at a table, eating soup.)

KUKLOV: I'm the prince.

ALMSGIVER: Oh, you're the prince!

KUKLOV: Yeah, I'm the prince. So what?

ALMSGIVER: I'll splash soup on you! *(Splashes soup.)*

KUKLOV: Don't!

ALMSGIVER: Why not?

KUKLOV: Why did you splash soup on me?

ALMSGIVER: What, you think because you're the prince you can't be splashed upon?

KUKLOV: That's exactly what I think!

ALMSGIVER: Well, I think the opposite.

KUKLOV: You think that, and I think this!

ALMSGIVER: I don't really care what you think.

KUKLOV: You're soulless.

ALMSGIVER: And your nose looks like a bathtub.

KUKLOV: And you have a face like you don't know where to sit!

ALMSGIVER: And you have a chicken's neck!

KUKLOV: And you're a pig.

ALMSGIVER: And I'll rip off your ears.

KUKLOV: And you're a pig.

ALMSGIVER: I'll rip off your ears!

KUKLOV: Pig.

ALMSGIVER: Really, a pig? Well, what are you then?

KUKLOV: I'm the prince.

ALMSGIVER: Oh, you're the prince!

KUKLOV: Yeah, I'm the prince. So what?

ALMSGIVER: I'll splash soup on you! *(Splashes soup.)*

(Etc.)

January 20, 1933.

A PLEAY

KOKA BRAINSKY: I'm getting married today.

MOTHER: Huh?

KOKA BRAINSKY: I'm getting married today.

MOTHER: What did you say?

KOKA BRAINSKY: I said, I'm getting married today.

MOTHER: What?

KOKA BRAINSKY: MAR-RIED. TO-DAY.

MOTHER: Mare? What about a mare?

KOKA BRAINSKY: Marriage! Mar-ri-age.

MOTHER: Porridge! What porridge?

KOKA BRAINSKY: No, not porridge. Mar-ri-age.

MOTHER: Why not porridge?

KOKA BRAINSKY: Yes, not porridge, that's what I mean!

MOTHER: Why not?

KOKA BRAINSKY: Not porridge! Do you understand? I didn't say porridge!

MOTHER: I don't see what porridge has to do with anything.

KOKA BRAINSKY: Goddamnit! Mare and porridge! What's wrong with you! You're speaking nonsense!

MOTHER: What about it?

KOKA BRAINSKY: Mare and porridge—I said—nonsense!

MOTHER: Not since what?

KOKA BRAINSKY: Not since?

MOTHER: Not since what?

KOKA BRAINSKY: What are you saying? Not since! Not since what?

MOTHER: There you go again… nonsense.

(KOKA BRAINSKY begins strangling his MOTHER just as his FIANCÉ enters the stage.)

April 1933.

UNTITLED (PYOTR MIKHAILOVICH)

PYOTR MIKHAILOVICH: This flower looks beautiful here. Or, maybe, better there? No, just like this, maybe, it's already very bright. And what if I switch off this lamp, and turn on that one? That's better. Now we'll put the butter here, and here we'll place the wine, then the glasses, then the vase, then the salt and pepper shakers, then a jar of jam, and then the bread. Very beautiful. She loves to eat. Now I must make it so it's only natural for her to sit in a certain chair. She sits there. And I sit as close as possible. I will put myself in this chair. I will have nowhere else to sit, and so I'll end up near her. When she arrives, I'll act as if I were still setting the table and didn't have time to arrange the chairs. All will occur very naturally. And later, when I end up near her, I'll say: "How lovely to sit with you." She'll say: "What's lovely about it?" I'll say: "You know, for me, just being with you is the most wonderful thing in the world. I am, it seems, a little bit in love with you." She'll say… Or, no, embarrassed, she'll simply blush or lower her head. And from there, I'll lean toward her and say: "You know, I just fell in love with you. Forgive me." If she's quiet again, I'll lean even closer… It would be better, of course, to move her to the sofa. But that might scare her. It must happen in the chairs. But I don't know—can I reach her? If she sits up straight, then, perhaps, but if she leans against the wall, then perhaps not. I'll say to her: "Maria Ivanovna, will you allow me to fall in love with you?"—no, that sounds dumb! It'd be better to say: "Maria Ivanovna! I'm glad that our friendship has become something else." No, that won't work either! In the end, I've got to kiss her, but I've got to do it gradually. Never kiss a girl without warning.

(Enter ILYA SEMYONOVICH.)

ILYA SEMYONOVICH: Petya, no one's visiting you today?

PYOTR MIKHAILOVICH: Someone's visiting, uncle.

ILYA SEMYONOVICH: Who?

PYOTR MIKHAILOVICH: A certain lady.

ILYA SEMYONOVICH: I was just now walking along the street and thinking, what if copper wire grew on our heads in place of hair?

PYOTR MIKHAILOVICH: So what, uncle?

ILYA SEMYONOVICH: So? That would be something! Just imagine: on your head, instead of hair, there's bright copper wire! You know, on you, it would be very fetching. Only not thin wire, but a very thick one. Better yet, not wire, but nails. Copper nails! And you know what? Better not copper, which resembles red hair, but platinum. Let's order such a wig!

PYOTR MIKHAILOVICH: I don't want to.

ILYA SEMYONOVICH: Oh, well. You've never had much taste. *(Overturning a vase.)* Ah!

PYOTR MIKHAILOVICH: Look, I have a guest arriving at any minute, and you've messed everything up—the tablecloth's soaking.

ILYA SEMYONOVICH: Hurry, Petya—take everything off the table. We'll rotate the tablecloth, and then put the tray here, over the spill.

PYOTR MIKHAILOVICH: Wait!—wait. We don't need to take everything off.

ILYA SEMYONOVICH: No, no, we need to rotate the tablecloth. Where should I put this?

(He puts the salad bowl on the floor.)

PYOTR MIKHAILOVICH: What are you doing?

ILYA SEMYONOVICH: Now. Now!

(He takes everything off the table.)

PYOTR MIKHAILOVICH: Uncle. Uncle! Leave it!

(The doorbell rings.)

That's her.

ILYA SEMYONOVICH: Hurry and turn the tablecloth around. *(He steps in the salad bowl, overturning it.)* Goddamnit! I stepped in the salad!

PYOTR MIKHAILOVICH: Why did you have to do all this!

ILYA SEMYONOVICH: Get me a dishrag! Everything's fine. Bring me a rag and go unlock the door.

(He bumps into a chair, which knocks against the table.)

PYOTR MIKHAILOVICH: Look, now you've spilled the sugar!

ILYA SEMYONOVICH: That's nothing. Hurry up and get me a rag!

PYOTR MIKHAILOVICH: This is a nightmare. *(He picks a plate up from the floor.)* What are you doing?

ILYA SEMYONOVICH: I spilled just a little bit of wine here, but I'll wipe it off the sofa with my handkerchief.

PYOTR MIKHAILOVICH: You better leave everything as it is. *(Doorbell rings again.)* Don't touch a thing! *(Runs to the door.)*

ILYA SEMYONOVICH: You tell her I'm your uncle, or better yet, say I'm your cousin… *(He takes the plates from the table and puts them on the sofa.)* Off with the tablecloth! Now I can put everything back. *(He throws the tablecloth on the floor and puts the dishes from the floor back on the table.)* Shit! The whole floor's covered in salad!

(Enter MARIA IVANOVNA in a coat, followed by PYOTR MIKHAILOVICH.)

PYOTR MIKHAILOVICH: Please come in, Maria Ivanovna. I'd like to introduce you to my uncle.

ILYA SEMYONOVICH: I'm Petya's uncle. Pleased to meet you. Petya and I didn't have time to set the table… Careful—there's salad on the floor over there!

MARIA IVANOVNA: Thank you.

PYOTR MIKHAILOVICH: I'll take your coat.

ILYA SEMYONOVICH: Allow me to help you.

PYOTR MIKHAILOVICH: Don't bother, uncle, I'm already helping Maria Ivanovna.

ILYA SEMYONOVICH: Sorry we haven't yet set the table. *(He tries to take a step forward but his legs are tangled in the tablecloth.)*

MARIA IVANOVNA: Don't fall! *(Laughs.)*

ILYA SEMYONOVICH: I'm sorry, I thought it was nothing, but then this tablecloth slid off the table… Petya, pick up that chair.

MARIA IVANOVNA: Hold on, I'll take off my shoes.

ILYA SEMYONOVICH: *(Moving to help PETYA pick up the chair.)* Allow me. I'm good at this.

PYOTR MIKHAILOVICH: Uncle, you'd better leave that chair in its place!

ILYA SEMYONOVICH: Okay, okay! *(He puts the chair back by the wall.)*

(Silence. All stand in place. A minute passes.)

ILYA SEMYONOVICH:
I like to wear my hair with a part.
I want to have a fence on my head.
I really want to have a fence on my head
that divides my hair in the middle. Like a part.

PYOTR MIKHAILOVICH: Well, uncle, you've just invented something very strange!

MARIA IVANOVNA: May I sit here?

PYOTR MIKHAILOVICH: Of course. Of course. Please sit!

ILYA SEMYONOVICH: Sit, of course! Of course!

PYOTR MIKHAILOVICH: Uncle!

ILYA SEMYONOVICH: Yeah yeah yeah.

(MARIA IVANOVNA sits on the sofa. UNCLE takes a hammer out of his mouth.)

PYOTR MIKHAILOVICH: What's that?

ILYA SEMYONOVICH: A little hammer.

MARIA IVANOVNA: What've you done? You took that out of your mouth?

ILYA SEMYONOVICH: No, no. I'm just killing time!

MARIA IVANOVNA: Is this magic?

(Silence.)

MARIA IVANOVNA: This is a bit awkward.

PYOTR MIKHAILOVICH: Now I'll set the table and it will be better.

MARIA IVANOVNA: No, Pyotr Mikhailovich, you're terrible!

PYOTR MIKHAILOVICH: Me! Why am I terrible?

MARIA IVANOVNA: Terrible! Terrible!

(UNCLE leaves the room on his tiptoes.)

MARIA IVANOVNA: Why did he leave on his tiptoes?

PYOTR MIKHAILOVICH: I'm very glad he left. *(He sets the table.)* Please forgive me for the mess.

MARIA IVANOVNA: When I began walking toward your place, I thought it'd be better not to come. It's best to follow these hunches.

PYOTR MIKHAILOVICH: On the contrary, I'm so happy you've come.

MARIA IVANOVNA: I don't know, I don't know.

PYOTR MIKHAILOVICH: The whole table covered in salad! And the sugar spilled, too! Do you hear how it scratches underfoot? It's gross. Tomorrow you'll tell everyone how it was at my place.

MARIA IVANOVNA: Well… Maybe I will tell someone.

PYOTR MIKHAILOVICH: Would you like a glass of wine?

MARIA IVANOVNA: No, thank you, but I'd love a piece of bread with cheese.

(He butters a slice of bread, puts a piece of cheese on it, and hands it over. She begins to eat.)

PYOTR MIKHAILOVICH: Would you like some tea?

MARIA IVANOVNA: No, I'd better not. I'd like to leave soon. I'll see myself out.

PYOTR MIKHAILOVICH: I don't know how to proceed. It's like I've got lockjaw.

MARIA IVANOVNA: Yes, yes, I'd better go.

PYOTR MIKHAILOVICH: No, I think you'd better not leave just yet. You must forgive me...

MARIA IVANOVNA: Why're you talking to me like that?

PYOTR MIKHAILOVICH: I'm talking to you like that on purpose. Deliberately.

MARIA IVANOVNA: No, this is all just awful.

PYOTR MIKHAILOVICH: Awful! Awful! Awful!

(Silence.)

PYOTR MIKHAILOVICH: I like this so much! It's lovely to sit this way with you.

MARIA IVANOVNA: Me too.

PYOTR MIKHAILOVICH: You're kidding, but I'm being serious. I honestly love it!

MARIA IVANOVNA: It's pretty chilly in here.

(She takes a hammer out of her mouth.)

PYOTR MIKHAILOVICH: What is that?

MARIA IVANOVNA: A little hammer.

PYOTR MIKHAILOVICH: What've you done? You took that out of your mouth!

MARIA IVANOVNA: All day this has been bothering me just here. *(Pointing to her throat.)*

PYOTR MIKHAILOVICH:

In my eyes, you see elongated sunbeams.
They stream like streams
and the whole garden rustles in my ears
and the branches rub against each other.

And the wind is heading to the heights
and your light eyes
like incomprehensible pitchers
I dream about at night. My god!

MARIA IVANOVNA:
Who are you speaking to?
I can't understand your speech.
You're just laughing at me.
You're a vulture, I'm a finch.
You're looking at me violently
and you're breathing too often…
Ah, don't look at me like that! Stop!
Are you listening? Can you hear me?

PYOTR MIKHAILOVICH: —

1933.

CHOP

(Summertime. A writing desk. A door on the right. A picture on the wall: a painting of a horse, and in the horse's mouth, a gypsy. OLGA PETROVNA is chopping wood. Each time she strikes the wood, her pince-nez fall off her nose. YEVDOKIM OSIPOVICH sits in an armchair, smoking.)

(OLGA PETROVNA strikes the log with an ax, which, however, doesn't splinter at all.)

YEVDOKIM OSIPOVICH: Chop!

(OLGA PETROVNA puts on her pince-nez, strikes the log.)

YEVDOKIM OSIPOVICH: Chop!

(OLGA PETROVNA puts on her pince-nez, strikes the log.)

YEVDOKIM OSIPOVICH: Chop!

(OLGA PETROVNA puts on her pince-nez, strikes the log.)

YEVDOKIM OSIPOVICH: Chop!

OLGA PETROVNA: *(Putting on her pince-nez.)* Yevdokim Osipovich! I beg you, stop saying that word, "chop."

YEVDOKIM OSIPOVICH: Okay, fine.

(OLGA PETROVNA strikes the log.)

YEVDOKIM OSIPOVICH: Chop!

OLGA PETROVNA: Yevdokim Osipovich! You promised to stop saying the "chop" word.

YEVDOKIM OSIPOVICH: Okay, okay, Olga Petrovna! I won't say it again.

(OLGA PETROVNA puts on her pince-nez, and strikes the log.)

YEVDOKIM OSIPOVICH: Chop!

OLGA PETROVNA: *(Putting on her pince-nez.)* Pathetic! An elderly man who can't understand a simple request!

YEVDOKIM OSIPOVICH: Olga Petrovna! Please, continue working. I won't bother you anymore.

OLGA PETROVNA: I beg you, seriously, I'm begging you. Let me at least chop this one log.

YEVDOKIM OSIPOVICH: Please, chop! Chop away, of course, chop!

(OLGA PETROVNA strikes the log.)

YEVDOKIM OSIPOVICH: Chop!

(OLGA PETROVNA drops the ax. She opens her mouth, but is unable to speak. YEVDOKIM OSIPOVICH gets up from his armchair, looks OLGA PETROVNA up and down, and slowly exits. OLGA PETROVNA stays frozen in place, watching him leave. Her mouth is wide open.)

(Curtains, slowly.)

1933.

THE HUNTERS

(Six men went hunting. Only four came back.)

(Therefore, two men did not come back.)

(WINDOWSON, GOATSON, STITCHSON, and MOTHSON came home safely, but WIDESON and HEELSON died on the hunt.)

(WINDOWSON had been hunting all day, he was sad and tired and didn't want to talk to anyone. GOATSON spent the whole day following WINDOWSON and pestering him with questions, which irritated WINDOWSON to no end.)

GOATSON: Want a smoke?

WINDOWSON: No.

GOATSON: *(Pointing.)* Want me to bring you that thing over there?

WINDOWSON: No!

GOATSON: Maybe you want me to tell you a joke?

WINDOWSON: No.

GOATSON: How about a drink? I have here some tea with cognac.

WINDOWSON: If you don't shut up, I'm gonna smack you upside the head with this rock and cut off your leg.

(WINDOWSON smacks GOATSON in the head with a rock and cuts off his leg. GOATSON falls to the ground.)

(Enter STITCHSON and MOTHSON. WINDOWSON hides in the bushes.)

STITCHSON & MOTHSON: What're you doing? What's going on?

GOATSON: Help me up!

MOTHSON: Don't worry. The wound will heal.

GOATSON: Where's Windowson?

WINDOWSON: I'm over here—not far!

GOATSON: My god! Oh god! Sa-a-a-ve me!

STITCHSON & MOTHSON: *(To GOATSON.)* There's no way he chopped off your leg.

WINDOWSON: Chopped it off and threw it over there!

STITCHSON: No, this is the Devil's work!

WINDOWSON: Wha-at?

STITCHSON: …work…

WINDOWSON: Wha-a-a?

STITCHSON: N…n…never mind.

GOATSON: How will I get home?

MOTHSON: Don't worry. We'll shove a branch in your stump.

STITCHSON: Can you stand on one leg?

GOATSON: Not well.

STITCHSON: Don't worry. We'll support you.

WINDOWSON: *(Pointing to GOATSON.)* Let me at him!

STITCHSON: It'd be better if you left.

WINDOWSON: No, let me! Let me! Let… me… I wanted to do this.

STITCHSON & MOTHSON: This is awful!

WINDOWSON: Ha ha ha!

MOTHSON: And where's Goatson now?

STITCHSON: He crawled into the bushes.

MOTHSON: You in there, Goatson? *(Rustles the bushes.)*

GOATSON: Shh, shh…!

MOTHSON: Look at what he's come to. Pathetic.

STITCHSON: What're we going to do with him?

MOTHSON: There's nothing you can do with him. I think we should just strangle him. Goatson!… Hey, Goatson! Can you hear me?

GOATSON: I can hear, but barely.

MOTHSON: Don't cry, brother. We're going to strangle you now. Hang on!

(WINDOWSON, MOTHSON, and STITCHSON all jump into the bushes. Sounds of struggling.)

There… There… There…

STITCHSON: Ok! Just a little more now!… a little more… that's it… that's it… And we're done!

(ALL THREE MEN emerge from the bushes, bedraggled but energized.)

MOTHSON: We're done!

WINDOWSON: Praise god!

THOMAS BOBROV AND HIS WIFE

A Comedy in Three Parts.

(GRANDMA is playing solitaire.)

GRANDMA: *(Drawing a card.)* These cards are coming out all wrong! A king? What am I supposed to do with a king? Just when I want a five, there's no five to be found. I need a five! Here it goes, come on now, show me a five! *(She draws another card.)* Damn it, the king again!

(She throws the cards across the table with such force that a porcelain vase falls and shatters.)

GRANDMA: Ah! Oh! Damnit! These are the devil's cards! *(She crawls under the table and picks up the pieces.)* This'll never glue back together. It was a good vase, too. A great vase. They don't make them like this anymore. Just one more piece. *(She stretches out.)*

(Enter BOBROV.)

BOBROV: Grandma! Why are you crawling under the table?

GRANDMA: It's fine, all fine. What do you need?

BOBROV: I came to ask whether I could trouble you for a spot of tea?

GRANDMA: Well, come on, help me up!

BOBROV: Did you drop something? Oh God, did you break the vase?!

GRANDMA: *(Mocking him.)* Oh god, did they break your face?

(BOBROV helps GRANDMA up. But as soon as he lets go of her, she falls back down on the floor.)

BOBROV: You fell down!

GRANDMA: I fell down, so what?

BOBROV: Let me help you up. *(He pulls GRANDMA up.)*

GRANDMA: My card game was going terribly. I tried and I tried, but… don't pull me up by the wrist like that, grab me from underneath my armpits… it was king after king. All I needed was a fiver and I kept getting the king. *(BOBROV lets go of GRANDMA and she falls again.)* Akh!

BOBROV: Oh God! You fell!

GRANDMA: Why do you keep saying that? I fell, I fell! What are you here for, anyway?

BOBROV: I came for a spot of tea.

GRANDMA: I know already. You said that. I hate hearing the same story twenty times over. You know… *(She falls again, and screams.)* I fell again and you want a spot of tea… well, what are you staring at, help me up!

BOBROV: *(Pulling GRANDMA up.)* Here, let me put you in the armchair, like this.

GRANDMA: Stop talking so much and lift me up correctly.

(BOBROV helps GRANDMA up.)

GRANDMA: Ah, I almost forgot, I've been meaning to tell you: my bedroom door, you know, isn't shutting properly again. I'm sure you had something to do with that.

BOBROV: No, I used screws to keep the door on its hinge.

GRANDMA: Do you think I know anything about hinges and screws? I don't care about that. I just want the door to shut.

BOBROV: It won't shut because the screws won't stay in the woodwork.

GRANDMA: Ok fine, fine. I'll let you deal with it. I just need to… Akh! *(GRANDMA falls off the armchair.)*

BOBROV: Oh God!

GRANDMA: Are you trying to hurt me? You think this is funny? You're useless! A useless lowlife! Just leave! Leave me alone.

BOBROV: No, Grandma, I was trying to put you in the armchair, honest!

GRANDMA: Did you hear what I said? Get out of here! Why are you still here? Why won't you leave me alone? Do you understand? Get out!

(Exit BOBROV.)

GRANDMA: That's right! Go on. Leave! Get the hell outta here! Useless lowlife!

(She gets up from the floor quite easily and sits in the armchair.)

GRANDMA: And his wife is a lowlife, too! She walks around naked acting like nothing's wrong, even in front of me, an old woman. She covers her crotch with the palm of her hand and walks around like that. And then she has the nerve to touch the bread with that hand. It's revolting! She thinks because she's young and pretty that she can do anything she likes. She doesn't even bathe properly! She says a woman should smell like a woman. When I see her coming I have to run to the bathroom and spray perfume up my nose. Maybe men like that kind of stink, but it disgusts me. Shameless lowlife. She walks around naked like it's no big deal! And when she sits down she doesn't close her legs, she lets everything hang out there in the open. And she's always wet down there. It's like she's leaking down there all the time. If you tell her to go wash herself, she'll say you shouldn't wash down there too often, and she'll take a napkin and wipe herself like it's no big deal. Well, if you're lucky she'll use a napkin, sometimes she just wipes herself with her hand, smearing it all over the place. I refuse to shake her hand. Her hands smell terrible. And her breasts are obscene. It's true they're firm and healthy, but they're so big, it's obscene. That's the wife Thomas found for himself. Why she hangs around him, I have no idea.

1933.

UNTITLED (THE END OF HISTORY)

VORONIN: *(Running.)*
The end of history!
People are running amok!
They're shooting at each other across the Neva!

STEPANOV: *(Jumping on a chair.)* What is the date today?

VORONIN: March nineteenth!

STEPANOV: *(Lying on the ground.)* I overslept! I overslept!

1933.

THE FALL, OR, THE KNOWLEDGE OF GOOD AND EVIL

(An alley lined with beautifully groomed trees is the garden of paradise. In the middle: the Tree of Life and the Tree of Knowledge of Good and Evil. In the background stands a church.)

FIGURA: *(Pointing at the tree.)* Behold the Tree of Knowledge of Good and Evil. You can eat the fruit from other trees, but the fruit of this tree you cannot eat.

ADAM: *(Pointing at the tree.)* Behold the Tree of Knowledge of Good and Evil. We will eat the fruit from other trees, but the fruit of this tree we will not eat. Eve, wait here for me, I'm going to pick raspberries.

(Exit ADAM.)

EVE: Behold the Tree of Knowledge of Good and Evil. Adam forbade me to eat the fruit of this tree. But I wonder, what does it taste like?

(Enter MASTER LEONARDO from behind a tree.)

MASTER LEONARDO: Eve! Here I come!

EVE: But tell me, Master Leonardo, why?

MASTER LEONARDO: You are so beautiful, so fair-skinned, and curvy. I've come here for your pleasure!

EVE: Good thinking!

MASTER LEONARDO: You know, Eve, I'm in love with you.

EVE: How should I know anything about that?

MASTER LEONARDO: Don't you know?

EVE: How should I know?

MASTER LEONARDO: Are you toying with me?

EVE: Oh, look, how funny! The he-pheasant is riding the she-pheasant like a horse!

MASTER LEONARDO: That's exactly what it is.

EVE: What what is?

MASTER LEONARDO: Love.

EVE: Love is hilarious! And you? You want to ride me like a horse?

MASTER LEONARDO: Yes, I do. But don't tell Adam.

EVE: Why would I?

MASTER LEONARDO: You're a good girl, I can tell.

EVE: I'm a tough broad.

MASTER LEONARDO: And do you love me?

EVE: Well, I wouldn't mind riding you around the garden.

MASTER LEONARDO: Climb on my shoulders.

(EVE mounts MASTER LEONARDO and rides him across the garden. Enter ADAM with a hat full of raspberries in his hand.)

ADAM: Eve? Where are you? Want some raspberries? Eve? Where did she go? I'll go find her!

(Exit ADAM.)

(Eve continues riding MASTER LEONARDO.)

EVE: *(Dismounting.)* Well, thanks. That was good for me.

MASTER LEONARDO: Now… eat this apple.

EVE: What's wrong with you! You can't eat the fruit of that tree.

MASTER LEONARDO: Listen, Eve! I learned the secrets of paradise long ago. I can tell you things…

EVE: Okay, go ahead. I'm listening.

MASTER LEONARDO: Will you listen to me?

EVE: I won't let you down.

MASTER LEONARDO: And you won't tell anyone else?

EVE: You can trust me.

MASTER LEONARDO: What if someone finds out?

EVE: Why would they?

MASTER LEONARDO: I believe you. You went to a good school. I've seen Adam, he's a pinhead.

EVE: He's unpolished.

MASTER LEONARDO: He's an idiot. He knows nothing. He hasn't traveled at all. He hasn't seen anything. He's been tricked, and now he's tricking you.

EVE: What do you mean?

MASTER LEONARDO: He forbids you from eating the fruit of this tree, but this is the most delicious fruit of all. And if you eat this fruit, you will know what's good and what's bad. You'll know so much that you'll be even smarter than God.

EVE: Is that possible?

MASTER LEONARDO: I'm telling you it is.

EVE: Well, now I don't know what to do.

MASTER LEONARDO: Eat this apple! Eat it! Eat it! Eat it!

(Enter ADAM with his hat.)

ADAM: Eve! Here you are!... And who's this?

(MASTER LEONARDO hides behind the bushes.)

ADAM: Who was that?

EVE: My friend, Master Leonardo.

ADAM: What did he want?

EVE: He let me mount him and ride him around the garden. It was hysterical.

ADAM: You didn't do anything else?

EVE: Nope.

ADAM: What is that in your hands?

EVE: This is an apple.

ADAM: From which tree?

EVE: This one.

ADAM: You're lying, it's from that one.

EVE: No, this one.

ADAM: You're lying.

EVE: You can trust me.

ADAM: I believe you.

SERPENT: *(Sitting in front of the Tree of Knowledge of Good and Evil.)* She's lying. Don't believe her. The apple is from that tree!

ADAM: Drop that apple!

EVE: No, you're a pinhead. You need to taste how delicious this fruit is.

ADAM: Eve, look...

EVE: There's nothing to look at!

ADAM: Have it your way then.

(EVE begins to eat the fruit. The SERPENT claps his hands.)

EVE: This is fantastic!... Only... wait... what's happening? You keep disappearing and reappearing again. Whoa! Everything disappears and then comes back again. How interesting everything is! Wow! I'm naked!... Adam, come a little closer, I want to mount you like a horse.

ADAM: What...

EVE: *(Handing ADAM the apple.)* Here, now you try it!

ADAM: I'm scared.

EVE: Eat it! Eat it! Eat it!

(ADAM eats the apple and immediately covers his penis with his hat.)

ADAM: I'm ashamed.

(FIGURA emerges from the church.)

FIGURA: You, he-creature, and you, she-creature, ate the forbidden fruit! Get out of my garden!

(FIGURA goes back into the church.)

ADAM: Where are we going to go now?

EVE: We're not going anywhere.

(An ANGEL with a sword of fire enters and chases ADAM and EVE out of the garden.)

ANGEL: Out! Out! Out! Get the hell out of here!

MASTER LEONARDO: *(Rising up from behind the bushes.)* Get out! Get out! Get out! Get out! *(Waves his hands.)* That's all! Curtains!

(Curtains.)

Dandan, September 27, 1934.

DISARMED, OR, FAILED LOVE

A Tragic Vaudeville in One Act.

LEV MARKOVICH: *(Running up to WOMAN.)* Let me in!

WOMAN: *(Pushing him away.)* Hey, back off!

LEV MARKOVICH: *(Shoves WOMAN to the ground.)* I said, let me in!

WOMAN: *(Trying to fend him off with her feet.)* Get off me!

LEV MARKOVICH: *(Groping her.)* C'mon, give it to me. Just this once…

WOMAN: *(Still trying to fend him off with her feet.)* Get off! Get off!

LEV MARKOVICH: Just one little thrust…

(WOMAN mumbles, says "no.")

LEV MARKOVICH: A thrust! One thrust!

(WOMAN rolls her eyes.)

(LEV MARKOVICH fusses about, reaches for his dick. He can't find it.)

LEV MARKOVICH: Hold on… *(Gropes himself.)* What the hell…

(WOMAN looks with surprise at LEV MARKOVICH.)

LEV MARKOVICH: Well, that's it.

WOMAN: What happened?

LEV MARKOVICH: Hm… *(Looks around, disoriented.)*

1934.

UNTITLED (AMERICA)

(An American street. AMERICANS walk to and fro. To the right there is a ticket booth. Above the ticket booth, a sign reads: MUSIC HALL, JAZZ ORCHESTRA UNDER THE DIRECTION OF MASTER WOODLEG AND HIS WIFE, THE BARONESS VON DER KLUKEN. The street is cluttered with advertisements. A line of Americans forms in front of a ticket booth. FENOROV enters and begins to look around. The Americans are dressed in rags.)

FENOROV: So this is it… America!… What luck! America!… I can't believe it!… America… Hey, you!… You, over there!… Is this really America?

AMERICAN: Ies, Amerika.

FENOROV: And this city is Chicago?

AMERICAN: Ies, Chikaga.

FENOROV: And you are an American?

AMERICAN: Amerikin.

FENOROV: *(In a deep voice.)* I can't believe my eyes!… And those people over there? Americans, too?

AMERICAN: Amerikins.

FENOROV: *(In falsetto.)* Wow!… *(In a deep voice.)* Americans!… *(Looks around.)* So there must be, you know, billionaires around here?

AMERICAN: Too many billionaires to count.

FENOROV: So if you're all billionaires—I mean, Americans—why are you all dressed in these rags?

AMERICAN: Because of this so-called crisis, man.

FENOROV: *(In falsetto.)* Wow!

AMERICAN: What's true is true.

FENOROV: *(In a deep voice.)* Can you believe it!

AMERICAN: Who are you, anyway?

FENOROV: Fenorov is my last name, and my social class is Khrentsch.

AMERICAN: Ah! So then, parlez-vous français?

FENOROV: What?

AMERICAN: Parlez-vous the French?

FENOROV: *(In falsetto.)* What you say!

AMERICAN: I said: do you speak le French?

FENOROV: I can't do what I can't do. As for American—we can speak that as much as you want. Really! Now, if you don't mind, good sir, tell me what's happening here? What's this line for? What product is being given away?

AMERICAN: This line is a line for nothing interesting. Nothing is being given away. This is the line to buy tickets.

FENOROV: *(In a falsetto.)* Yippee!

AMERICAN: This is a music hall, man. There will be a jazz performance under the direction of the illustrious Master Woodleg and his famed wife, Baron von der Kluken's daughter.

FENOROV: *(In a deep voice.)* What luck! Thank you, thank you, thank you! I want a ticket! *(Gets in line.)*

> *(A long line of Americans dressed in torn, dirty clothing waits at the ticket booth of the music hall.)*

FENOROV: Who's last in line here?

GUY: Where do you think you're going? Get in line!

FENOROV: I just asked where the line ends.

GUY: You got a thing for asking, huh?

FENOROV: *(Touching the elbow of GAL.)* Who's last?

GAL: Don't touch me! I'm standing behind this guy.

GUY: I'm not a guy! I'm the king of breath mints!

FENOROV: *(In falsetto.)* What luck!

GAL: Well whoop-de-doo, I'm the queen of dog hair.

FENOROV: *(In a deep voice.)* Fascinating!

GUY: Well I don't care who you are!

GAL: You are quite the conversationalist, breath mint!

GUY: Dog hair!

A CIRCUS NUMBER

(A fight ensues. QUEEN OF DOG HAIR is taking it out on THE KING OF BREATH MINTS. The other AMERICANS run around, yelling: "He's gonna beat her!" "She's gonna beat him!")

(The Music Hall doors open. The stage and the auditorium are visible. Ragged AMERICANS and FENOROV run inside and take their seats. All are shouting and yelling. Both the stage and the auditorium are visible. The hall becomes silent. The RING LEADER, dressed in circus clothing, enters.)

RING LEADER: Ladies and Gentlemen! We, being the Americans, know how to have fun! But how am I supposed to make you laugh, you animals? You've got chewing tobacco and your gum and all you do is spit!… Could anything make you laugh?… No way!… It's impossible!…

AMERICANS: *(In unison.)* Walla walla walla! Walla walla walla! Make us laugh!

RING LEADER: But how can I? Do I know how?

AMERICANS: Walla walla walla!

RING LEADER: Should I make funny faces?

AMERICANS: Faces! Faces!

(The RING LEADER makes faces. The AMERICANS laugh.)

AMERICANS: *(Laughing loudly.)* Ha ha ha!… Oh that's funny! Oh oh oh that's so funny!

RING LEADER: Are you entertained?

AMERICANS: Do it again! Again!

RING LEADER: That's enough, children! Now the Jazz Orchestra will perform under the direction of Master Woodleg...

AMERICANS: *(Laughing loudly.)* Bravo! Bravo! Whoopee! Hee-hee!

RING LEADER: And in the orchestra, the Baroness von der Kluken will perform with her lovely children!

(Applause.)

(Exit RING LEADER. Curtain. FENOROV keeps talking in the audience.)

FENOROV: What happens next?

KING OF BREATH MINTS: *(Jumping out of his seat.)* It's this guy again!

QUEEN OF DOG HAIR: Breath Mint again!

(The KING sits down.)

KING OF BREATH MINTS: *(Wringing his fists.)* Why I oughta!!

(Curtain rises.)

1934.

UNTITLED (THE BARON)

(The garden at the castle of the BARON VON DER BUNDER-HANGEL-HINGEL. There's a fence to the right of the castle, behind which is the dacha of the professor TATARINMAN. The BARON'S WIFE is sitting in an armchair and the BARON is standing in front of his WIFE. Roosters and hens walk across the garden and cluck from time to time.)

BARON: He's a professor?

WIFE: A professor.

BARON: His surname is Tatarinman?

WIFE: Tatarinman.

BARON: He bought that house?

WIFE: He bought it.

BARON: Near my house?

WIFE: Near your house.

BARON: In our county, do I, the Baron von der Bunder-Hangel-Hingel, occupy a superior position?

WIFE: A position.

BARON: And has this upstart, having bought himself a house near my house, made me a visit?

WIFE: He did.

BARON: What do you mean, he did?

WIFE: Ach, no, he didn't! He didn't!... Have a candy.

BARON: *(Taking a candy.)* Exactly! The devil didn't! That's it exactly! And I! I! Can I put up with this?

WIFE: Nope.

1934.

PUSHKIN AND GOGOL

(GOGOL falls onto the stage from behind the curtains and lies down.)

PUSHKIN: *(Walks on stage, trips over GOGOL and falls.)* Damnit! Is that Gogol?

GOGOL: *(Standing up.)* This is so exhausting! He won't leave me alone. *(Walks away, trips over PUSHKIN and falls down.)* I tripped over Pushkin!

PUSHKIN: *(Standing up.)* There's no end to it! *(Walks away, trips over GOGOL and falls down.)* Damn! Gogol again!

GOGOL: *(Standing up.)* He's always in my way! *(Walks away, trips over PUSHKIN and falls down.)* This is so exhausting! I tripped over Pushkin again!

PUSHKIN: *(Standing up.)* How absurd! Nonsense! *(Walks away, trips over GOGOL and falls down.)* Over Gogol!

GOGOL: *(Standing up.)* What cruel mockery! What a sham! *(Walks away, trips over PUSHKIN and falls down.)* Pushkin again!

PUSHKIN: *(Standing up.)* Damn! Seriously, damn! *(Walks away, trips over GOGOL and falls down.)* Over Gogol!

GOGOL: *(Standing up.)* There's no escape! Literally none! *(Walks away, trips over PUSHKIN and falls down.)* Over Pushkin!

PUSHKIN: *(Standing up.)* Damn and damn again! *(Walks away, trips over GOGOL and falls down.)* Gogol!

GOGOL: *(Standing up.)* There's no way out! *(Walks off the stage.)*

(From behind the curtain, yells:)

Pushkin!

(Curtains.)

1934.

A FAILED PERFORMANCE

(PETRAKOV-GORBUNOV enters the stage. He tries to speak, but hiccups. He vomits. He exits.)

(Enter PRITYKIN.)

PRITYKIN: His honor, Petrakov-Gorbunov, will be… *(He vomits and runs away.)*

(Enter MAKAROV.)

MAKAROV: Pritykin… *(He vomits and runs away.)*

(Enter SERPUKHOV.)

SERPUKHOV: In order to… *(He vomits and runs away.)*

(Enter KUROVA.)

KUROVA: I should… *(He vomits and runs away.)*

(Enter LITTLE GIRL, running.)

LITTLE GIRL: Daddy wanted me to tell you that the theater is closed. Everyone is sick!

(Curtains.)

1934.

A DUET: DERBANTOVA AND KUKUSHIN-DERGUNOV

DERBANTOVA: *(Running through the garden and pointing her finger in different directions.)* Zhik! Zhik! Zhik!

KUKUSHIN-DERGUNOV: What's with you, Anna Pavlovna, are you batshit?

DERBANTOVA: Zhik! Zhik! Zhik!

KUKUSHIN-DERGUNOV: Anna Pavlovna.

DERBANTOVA: *(Suddenly standing still.)* Huh?

KUKUSHIN-DERGUNOV: I'm saying that you, Anna Pavlovna, have gone crazy.

DERBANTOVA: No.

KUKUSHIN-DERGUNOV: No what?

DERBANTOVA: I haven't gone crazy.

KUKUSHIN-DERGUNOV: How is that possible?

DERBANTOVA: Look at me, I'm not crazy!

KUKUSHIN-DERGUNOV: Strange.

DERBANTOVA: Very.

KUKUSHIN-DERGUNOV: *(After thinking carefully.)* Anna Pavlovna!

DERBANTOVA: Huh?

KUKUSHIN-DERGUNOV: Don't you see, Anna Pavlovna, you're not a kid anymore, and neither am I.

DERBANTOVA: I'm younger than you are.

KUKUSHIN-DERGUNOV: Well, yeah, of course you're younger!

DERBANTOVA: Well, it's the same thing!

KUKUSHIN-DERGUNOV: *(Turning and bowing to the audience.)* The first act is now complete.

DERBANTOVA: Now, we'll begin the second act.

KUKUSHIN-DERGUNOV: Let's begin!

DERBANTOVA: *(Pointing her finger in different directions.)* Zhik! Zhik! Zhik!

KUKUSHIN-DERGUNOV: You're too old to be clowning around, Anna Pavlovna.

1930-1934.

THE DIFFERENCE IN HEIGHT BETWEEN HUSBAND AND WIFE

HUSBAND: I whipped my daughter and now I'm going to beat my wife.

WIFE & DAUGHTER: *(From behind the door.)* Babababababababab! Hee haw hee haw hee haw hee haw hee haw!

HUSBAND: Ivan! Butler!!!! Ivan!

(Enter IVAN. IVAN has no hands.)

IVAN: Sir, at your service!

HUSBAND: Ivan! Where are your hands?

IVAN: During the great war, I lost them in the heat of battle!

1930-1934.

ADAM AND EVE

A Vaudeville in Four Parts.

Admission is 30 rubles.

ACT ONE

ANTON ISAAKOVICH: I don't want to be Anton anymore. I want to be Adam. And you, Natalia, you will be Eve.

NATALIA BORISOVNA: *(Sitting on the fence and eating halva.)* Are you an idiot?

ANTON ISAAKOVICH: I'm not an idiot. I'm Adam, and you're Eve.

NATALIA BORISOVNA: *(Looks right and left.)* Uhh… I don't get it…

ANTON ISAAKOVICH: It's easy! Here, look, we'll stand on the table, and when someone comes in we'll say, "Allow us to introduce ourselves: We are Adam and Eve."

NATALIA BORISOVNA: You're insane. You're crazy!

ANTON ISAAKOVICH: *(Climbing on the table and pulling NATALIA BORISOVNA up by the hand.)* Look, we'll stand here and bow to anyone who comes.

NATALIA BORISOVNA: *(Climbing on the desk.)* But, why? Why!

ANTON ISAAKOVICH: Wait… did you hear that? Someone's coming. Get ready.

(SOMEONE knocks at the door.)

ANTON ISAAKOVICH: Come in!

(Enter WEISSBREM.)

ANTON ISAAKOVICH & NATALIA BORISOVNA: *(Bowing.)* Allow us to introduce ourselves: We are Adam and Eve!

(WEISSBREM is struck by lightning.)

(Curtains.)

ACT TWO

(Along the streets the people are jumping on three legs. From Moscow, a violent wind blows.)

(Curtains.)

ACT THREE

(ADAM ISAAKOVICH and EVE BORISOVNA fly across the Leningrad sky. The people fall to their knees and cry for mercy. ADAM ISAAKOVICH and EVE BORISOVNA politely smile.)

(Curtains.)

ACT FOUR: THE FINALE

(ADAM and EVE perch in a birch tree and sing.)

(Curtains.)

February 23, 1935.

UNTITLED (ELIZABETH AND CHESTNUT)

CHESTNUT: Liza! I'm begging you, please. Tell me who you are!

ELIZABETH: Are you going to leave me alone or not?

CHESTNUT: No! I cannot! I can't!

ELIZABETH: You can't what?

CHESTNUT: Liza! Who are you?

ELIZABETH: You're so fixated on that idiotic question. Do you know who I am or not?

CHESTNUT: I don't know! I really don't!

UNTITLED (GREGORY AND SIMON)

GREGORY: *(Punching SIMON in the face.)* Look, winter's here and it's time to light the fire. What say you?

SIMON: I say, if what you say about winter is true, then, perhaps, yes, it's time to light the fire.

GREGORY: *(Punching SIMON in the face.)* Will this winter be cold or warm? What say you?

SIMON: Well, perhaps, considering the fact that summer was rainy, the winter will be cold. If summer is wet, winter is always cold.

GREGORY: *(Punching SIMON in the face.)* Ah, well I don't feel cold.

SIMON: You're correct to say you don't feel cold. Such is your nature.

GREGORY: *(Punching SIMON in the face.)* I never freeze!

SIMON: Ouch!

GREGORY: *(Punching SIMON in the face.)* Ouch what?

SIMON: *(Holding his face.)* Ouch! My face hurts!

GREGORY: *(Grabbing SIMON'S face.)* Why does it hurt?

SIMON: *(Falling off of his chair.)* Ouch! I don't know.

GREGORY: *(Kicking SIMON in the face.)* Well, personally, I feel fine.

SIMON: *(Trying to stand up.)* You sombitch, I'll teach you how to fight!

GREGORY: *(Punching SIMON in the face.)* I'm the teacher!

SIMON: *(Falling on his back.)* Piece of shit!

GREGORY: Don't you ever tell me to shit!

SIMON: *(Trying to stand up.)* I've had it with you, brother. It's clear we can't be friends and it's your fault!

GREGORY: *(Digging his heel into SIMON'S mouth.)* Speak! Say something! Let's hear it!

SIMON: *(Falling on his back.)* Ahk!

(*Enter LANEV.)*

LANEV: What's all this about?

1935.

UNTITLED (NINA AND BARBARA)

NINA: You know! A? You know? No? Have you heard? A?

BARBARA MIKHAILOVNA: What is it? A? What is it?

NINA: No, just think! Barbara Mikhailovna! Just think!

BARBARA MIKHAILOVNA: What is it? A? What is it?

NINA: —Yes, you already know, Barbara Mikhailovna! You already know!

BARBARA MIKHAILOVNA: Yes, what is it! At long last, what is it?!

NINA: No no, listen, Barbara Mikhailovna! Ha-ha-ha.

BARBARA MIKHAILOVNA: Yes, I'm listening, I'm listening! What is it?

NINA: Ha-ha-ha! And also the Queen!

BARBARA MIKHAILOVNA: What nonsense!

NINA: Definitely the Queen!

BARBARA MIKHAILOVNA: This is nonsense!

NINA: Our Queen! The world's! The old buzzard! And over there!

BARBARA MIKHAILOVNA: Where's there?

NINA: Yes, all over there, dammit! He's hung up on Elizaveta!

BARBARA MIKHAILOVNA: Hung up?

NINA: Yes, he fell in love!

BARBARA MIKHAILOVNA: Who fell in love? Are you crazy?

NINA: Look, Vladimir's gone crazy! Sergei's gone crazy…

BARBARA MIKHAILOVNA: There's nothing interesting about that!

NINA: Eddy's gone completely crazy…

BARBARA MIKHAILOVNA: There's nothing interesting about that!

NINA: Where's the fun in that! There's nothing interesting!

BARBARA MIKHAILOVNA: I just don't understand, why are all men crazy?

NINA: It's not very attractive!

BARBARA MIKHAILOVNA: It's just ugly!

NINA: None of this is interesting.

BARBARA MIKHAILOVNA: Nothing is interesting!

1934-1936.

LEONIDOV AND GRIGORIEV

LEONIDOV: I maintain that when we approached him, he walked away, and then he left.

GRIGORIEV: Yes, he left, but not then.

LEONIDOV: He definitely left then. At first he walked away, and then he left.

GRIGORIEV: What are you saying? When he left he left, but it wasn't later.

LEONIDOV: We walked up to him?

GRIGORIEV: Yes.

LEONIDOV: He walked away?

GRIGORIEV: Yes.

LEONIDOV: And then he left!

GRIGORIEV: Oh, here we go again! He didn't leave then! My God, it wasn't then!

LEONIDOV: Cry as long as you like! But he walked away, and then he left!

GRIGORIEV: Not then.

LEONIDOV: It was then!

GRIGORIEV: It wasn't, because he walked away, but he didn't leave then!

LEONIDOV: Well, that's your opinion! And mine is that he left.

GRIGORIEV: —

1934-1936.

THE SERVER

(A restaurant. PETE enters and sits down at a table. A SERVER enters with a menu, and places it in front of PETE. PETE looks over the menu for a long time. The SERVER stands silently near him.)

PETE: Give me, if you will, the boeuf-buoy.

SERVER: What would you like, sir?

PETE: If possible, the boeuf-buoy.

SERVER: What did you say, sir?

PETE: *(Shyly.)* I said *(Clears his throat.)* give me the boeuf-buoy.

SERVER: *(Leaning in.)* What do you want?

PETE: *(Timidly.)* Give me the boeuf…

(The SERVER leans back. PETE flinches and is silent.)

SERVER: So. What do you want?

PETE: I would like, if it's possible…

SERVER: What?

PETE: Boeuf-buoy, boeuf-buoy.

SERVER: Huh?

PETE: Boeuf…

SERVER: Boeuf?

PETE: *(Excited.)* Buoy!

SERVER: *(Surprised.)* Buoy?

PETE: *(Nodding rapidly.)* Boeuf-buoy. Boeuf-buoy.

SERVER: *(Stroking his chin as if thinking deeply.)* Boeuf-buoy?

PETE: If it's possible…

(The SERVER stands in contemplation, stroking his chin and scratching his head. PETE pulls himself closer to the table. The SERVER exits. Silence.)

(A SECOND SERVER enters with a menu, and places it in front of PETE. PETE looks over the menu for a long time. The SERVER stands silently near him.)

PETE: Give me, if you will, the boeuf-buoy.

SERVER: What would you like, sir?

PETE: If possible, the boeuf-buoy.

SERVER: What did you say, sir?

PETE: *(Shyly.)* I said *(Clears his throat)* give me the boeuf-buoy.

SERVER: *(Leaning in.)* What do you want?

PETE: *(Timidly.)* Give me the boeuf…

(The server leans back. Pete flinches and becomes silent. Minutes pass. Silence.)

SERVER: So. What do you want?

PETE: I would like, if it's possible…

SERVER: What?

PETE: Boeuf-buoy, boeuf-buoy.

SERVER: Huh?

PETE: Boeuf…

SERVER: Boeuf?

PETE: *(Excited.)* Buoy!

SERVER: *(Surprised.)* Buoy?

PETE: *(Nodding rapidly.)* Boeuf-buoy. Boeuf-buoy.

SERVER: *(Stroking his chin as if thinking deeply.)* Boeuf-buoy?

PETE: If it's possible…

(The SERVER stands for a long time in contemplation, stroking his chin and scratching his head. PETE pulls himself closer to the table. The SERVER exits.)

(A THIRD SERVER enters with a menu, and places it in front of PETE. PETE looks over the menu for a long time. The SERVER stands silently near him.)

1935-1936.

EVSTIGNEEV'S LAUGH

A Vaudeville for Three Voices.

Characters:
EVSTIGNEEV
FIRST VOLODYA
SECOND VOLODYA
EVDOKIA – wife of Evstigneev
VERA ALEKSANDROVNA SULIPANOVA – Evdokia's cousin
JANITOR PYOTR PERETS
JANITRESS
LOVE AFFAIRS, ZEBRAS, and CLASSICAL GIRLS

ACT ONE

(EVSTIGNEEV stands in the middle of a room and tries to make a sound on a flute. EVSTIGNEEV'S wife EVDOKIA kneels in front of him.)

EVDOKIA: Evstigneev! My dear husband! My spouse! Beloved person and friend! Evstigneev! I beg you not to blow into the flute! Evstigneev!

EVSTIGNEEV: *(Laughs.)* He-he-he!

EVDOKIA: Evstigneev! Four and a half years you've blown into that flute and you still can't make a sound! Give it up! I am on my knees before you! You see? I kiss your feet. Can't you hear me? You're an evil, no-good man, Evstigneev! I slave away day and night so we don't starve. I am a servant: I run to the shops, I prepare dinner, wash the dishes, clean the room, do your laundry… Do you see what my hands look like now? I am sick and unhappy, doing this impossible work for you. And you? You blow on your flute! And perhaps if there were some use… But not only can you not play any songs, you can't even make a sound! Wake up! Wake up, Evstigneev!

EVSTIGNEEV: *(Laughs.)* He-he-he!

EVDOKIA: No, I can't do it anymore! This isn't a man, but some kind of beast!

(She rises from her knees.)

Listen, Evstigneev! I've done everything I can to reason with you. Nothing works. I'm weak and can't take the flute away from you myself. You beat me. So I've decided to resort to extreme measures. Do you hear what I'm saying, Evstigneev? You hear?

EVSTIGNEEV: *(Blows into his flute.)* Foo-foo-foo!

EVDOKIA: So you hear what I'm saying to you? Ah, well! You don't want to listen! Okay: now I'll resort to that extreme measure I told you about. Not listening? Okay! I'll call the janitor!

(EVSTIGNEEV stops blowing into his flute.)

EVDOKIA: You heard? Now I'll call the janitor.

EVSTIGNEEV: Why?

EVDOKIA: So the janitor can help me take away your flute, break it, and throw it in the trash.

EVSTIGNEEV: No? He-he-he!

EVDOKIA: Not "no," but yes.

EVSTIGNEEV: How's that?

(He regards his flute and tries to blow into it.)

EVDOKIA: Ah, you again! Well, okay…

(Knock at the door. EVSTIGNEEV and EVDOKIA listen silently. The knock repeats.)

EVDOKIA: Who's there?

VOICE AT THE DOOR: Dorochka! It's me! Open up, s'il-vous-plaît!

EVDOKIA: Ah, it's you, Vera! Just a minute. *(To EVSTIGNEEV.)* Hide your flute!

EVSTIGNEEV: *(Laughs.)* He-he-he!

EVDOKIA: Hand the flute over! Hand the flute over this minute!

EVSTIGNEEV: *(Hiding the flute behind his back.)* He-he!

EVDOKIA: Just a minute, Verochka! *(To EVSTIGNEEV.)* Will you give me the flute? Oh well!…

(She walks to the door and opens it.)

Come in Verochka!

(Enter VERA ALEKSANDROVNA SULIPANOVA.)

EVDOKIA: Let me introduce you: Evstigneev, my husband. And this is Vera Aleksandrovna Sulipanova, my cousin.

SULIPANOVA: *(Approaching EVSTIGNEEV.)* Nice to meet you!

EVSTIGNEEV: He-he-he!

EVDOKIA: Sit down over here, Vera, and tell me how you've been.

(SULIPANOVA sits, putting her feet up on a chair.)

SULIPANOVA: O, my goodness, there's so much news! I'm mad for the theater and the high life. Yes, dearest, I'm all for society! Gregor gave me the most delicate foreign stocking, but, unfortunately, only one. So it can't be worn. But when I have guests over, I throw this stocking on the sofa, as if I'd forgotten to pick it up, and so, of course, they think I have the pair. Borman saw this stocking and said, "You can't throw these stockings around!" And I said to him: "Oh! I have a whole bunch! But no shoes!…" Ah, yes, dearest, je suis malade, my armpit hurts. This Harry licked my arm up to the collar, but I didn't let him get farther than my armpits. I didn't let Harry catch me!

EVSTIGNEEV: He-he!

SULIPANOVA: Oy! I shouldn't be saying such things in the presence of a man. But, all the same, you're the husband of my cousin and anyhow we people of high society can allow ourselves a few frivolities.

EVSTIGNEEV: He-he! *(Blows into his flute.)*

SULIPANOVA: What's that?

EVDOKIA: You see, my husband wants to play the flute.

SULIPANOVA: Good heavens! Why?

EVDOKIA: Ah, Vera! All day he plagues me with this flute. You see? So it goes from morning to evening.

SULIPANOVA: Well, hide the thing from him.

EVDOKIA: —

1935-1936.

UNTITLED (FEDYA #1)

— Fedya, hey, Fedya?

— What's up?

— Oh, I'll show you what's up!

(Silence.)

— Fedya, hey, Fedya?

— What's the matter?

— You sombitch! And you ask me what's the matter!

—What do you want from me?

—Are you hearing this? What do I want from him!… You know what I could do to you—you bastard—for asking that… I could throw you so hard you'll fly all the way to you know where!

— Where?

— Into the pot.

(Silence.)

UNTITLED (FEDYA #2)

— Fedya, hey Fedya?

— What's with you, auntie, are you crazy?

— Ah! Oh! Say that again, what you just said!

— I won't say it again.

— Yeah, that's what I thought! Know your place! Or else! And moreover!

February 23, 1937.

EXTENSIVE RESEARCH

YERMOLAYEV: I just saw Blinov showing off his strength. I've never seen anything so powerful. He's strong as a bear! He's terrifying to look at! He lifted a table, swung it over his head, and threw it almost twenty feet!

DOCTOR: I would love to research that kind of strength. Of course, we scientists know that such specimens exist, but we cannot explain why or how. At the moment, we are unable to determine the source of such strength with any degree of certainty. Will you introduce me to Blinov? I'll give him a research pill.

YERMOLAYEV: What kind of pill?

DOCTOR: I'm not going to give him a pill.

YERMOLAYEV: You just said you wanted to give him a pill.

DOCTOR: No, I didn't. You misheard me. I didn't say anything about a pill.

YERMOLAYEV: With all due respect, doctor, I just heard you say something about a pill.

DOCTOR: Nope.

YERMOLAYEV: What do you mean, nope?

DOCTOR: I didn't say that.

YERMOLAYEV: You didn't say what?

DOCTOR: You said it.

YERMOLAYEV: What did I say?

DOCTOR: You were saying something. I believe you interrupted yourself. Please, go on.

YERMOLAYEV: Go on?

DOCTOR: Don't be ashamed. This sort of verbal ineptitude—choking on words, struggling to finish sentences—is common among people like you. You speak too quickly. It makes you stutter.

YERMOLAYEV: I didn't stutter. I-I-I d-d-don't s-s-stutter.

DOCTOR: You're mistaken. Can't you tell? You're already blushing. And your hands—aren't they cold?

YERMOLAYEV: No, w-w-why would they be cold?

DOCTOR: Just as I suspected! And look! You're having difficulty breathing. Please, sit down. Just relax. Good, good. It's alright. Just relax.

YERMOLAYEV: What is…

DOCTOR: Shh, don't strain your voice. You'll need your strength. Don't worry, I'll make all of the pain go away.

YERMOLAYEV: Doctor! You're scaring me!

DOCTOR: I'm helping you, my friend. Here, swallow this pill. Swallow it!

(The DOCTOR shoves a pill into YERMOLAYEV'S mouth.)

YERMOLAYEV: *(Coughing.)* Ugh. Gross. It's disgustingly sweet. What's it for?

DOCTOR: Nothing. Don't worry. It's a guaranteed cure.

YERMOLAYEV: I feel hot… Doctor, your face is green…

DOCTOR: Yes, good good. Relax, friend. In a minute or two, you'll be dead.

YERMOLAYEV: What? Doctor, please! I can't! Doctor! What—? Please!

DOCTOR: You swallowed the research pill.

YERMOLAYEV: Please *(Coughs.)* help me! *(Coughs.)* Help! I can't. Help… breathe…

(YERMOLAYEV goes limp.)

DOCTOR: There he goes. Not a breath left in him. I officially declare this man dead. He died without finding the answers to life's greatest questions. He died alone and confused. In the face of such obstacles, we scientists must press on. We must continue to research the mysteries of death.

June 21, 1937.

UNTITLED (ANYTHING MEANINGFUL ON EARTH)

ME: Is there anything meaningful on earth which could change the course of history, not only in this world, but in other worlds, too?

TEACHER: There is!

ME: Well… what is it?

TEACHER: Well…

ME: I'm waiting…

TEACHER:…

ME: I'm patiently waiting…

(Silence.)

ME: I'm patiently waiting and standing still…

TEACHER: Ho-la-la!

ME: We're both standing still!

TEACHER: Ho-le-le!

ME: Yes, yes, we're both being quiet and standing still!

July 16-17, 1937.

SHAMELESS: AN OPERA IN FOUR ACTS

ACT I, SCENE I

(An empty stage. Mountains are painted across so a man can run from the mountains with a samovar in his arms. There are two chairs on the stage.)

(BOGOLYUBOV stands on the stage, holding a cane in his hand. Across from BOGOLYUBOV stands POROSHKOV. The actors sing throughout.)

BOGOLYUBOV: *(Singing.)* Well, now I'll hit you!

POROSHKOV: *(Singing.)* No, you won't hit me!

BOGOLYUBOV: No, I'll hit you!

POROSHKOV: However, you won't!

BOGOLYUBOV: I will!

POROSHKOV: You won't!

(Both sit on the chairs.)

CHORUS I: He'll hit him.

CHORUS II: No, he won't hit him.

BOGOLYUBOV: *(Standing.)* Now I'll hit you.

(He strikes POROSHKOV with his cane, but POROSHKOV dodges the blow.)

1934-1937.

EVERYDAY HAPPENINGS: A VAUDEVILLE

SNO: Hellow! Eh, let's get drunk! Eh, let's hit the town! Eh! Eh! Eh!

MARSHA: What the hell's wrong with you? Eddy Edwardovich?

SNO: Eh! I wanna get drunk! Let's hit the town!

MARSHA: Calm down, Eddy Edwardovich, please relax for a minute. Would you like me to make you some tea?

SNO: Tea? What? No! I wanna pound some vodka!

MARSHA: Eddy Edwardovich, what's the matter with you. I don't understand.

SNO: Oh, then dun try a-understand! Gah, woman… more vodka!

MARSHA: Jesus! What's the matter with you?… Danya! Danya!

KHARMS: *(Lying on the floor.)* Yeah? What now?

MARSHA: What should I do about this guy? Why's he acting like this?

SNO: Eh, let's hit the town! (*He takes a shot of vodka and blows it out of his nose.)*

MARSHA: *(Hiding behind the piano.)* Oh Holy Mother! Sweet Virgin Mother of Christ!

KHARMS: *(Lying on the floor.)* Hey, you, yes, it's true, prayer can be a little confusing…

SNO: *(He reaches for another bottle and breaks the cupboard door.)* Eh… the town!

(Curtains.)

(Sounds of MARSHA scratching her head.)

(Faith, Hope, Charity, and Wisdom.)

September 30, 1938.

GRANDPA AND THE TURNIP: A BALLET

(The stage is empty. Something sticks out of the ground. It looks like a turnip. The music is playing. A bird flies over the river. On the right side of the stage stands a motionless figure. A DWARF enters. Gently he strokes his beard. Music is playing. The DWARF stomps his little feet. He stomps them again. He begins to dance.

He sings: "Yippee, I planted a turnip—la la la la la!" He dances and sings. The bird is flying. The bird is still flying. The DWARF throws his hat on the ground and goes inside, and again begins to sing, "I planted a turnip, I planted a turnip—la la la la la!" On the right side of the stage, a large book opens. There, DUKE and ANDREI SEMYONOVICH sit on the balcony. They drink tea. ANDREI SEMYONOVICH is wearing gold pince-nez. They drink tea. On the table is a samovar.)

DUKE: He planted it, but we pull it out. Right?

ANDREI SEMYONOVICH: *(Laughs in a deep voice.)* Right!

DUKE: *(Laughs in an even deeper voice.)* Right!

(Down below: the DWARF dances away. The music fades to a hum.)

(Up high: DUKE and ANDREI SEMYONOVICH laugh and make funny faces at each other. They put up their dukes. DUKE puts his dukes over his head. ANDREI puts his dukes below the table.)

(Down below: "Yankee Doodle Dandy" begins to play. An AMERICAN enters, pulling a tiny Ford Truck on a string. He begins to dance around the turnip.)

(Up high: DUKE and ANDREI SEMYONOVICH stare with their mouths wide open. The music stops. The AMERICAN stops.)

DUKE: What kind of nut job is this?

ANDREI SEMYONOVICH: That is, well, how can I put this delicately… America?

(Again the music begins to play.)

(Down below: The AMERICAN begins to dance. He dances toward the turnip. He tries to pull the turnip out of the ground. The music fades.)

DUKE: *(From up high.)* He's so weak!

ANDREI SEMYONOVICH: Shh! Don't say that so loudly, Selifan Mitrofanovich, you'll offend him!

(The music begins to play loudly.)

(Down below: AUNTY ENGLAND comes swimming into the scene. On the legs of battleships, in the arms of parachutes. She dances toward the turnip. The AMERICAN begins to examine the turnip more carefully.)

DUKE: *(From up high.)* And who's this, Holland?

ANDREI SEMYONOVICH: *(Offended.)* Not Holland, England!

DUKE: Pull it up, or you'll be sent to the labor camp!

ANDREI SEMYONOVICH: Shhh. *(Looks around, hoping no one heard.)*

(The music is full blast.)

(Down below: FRANCE enters the stage, running and yelling: "Eh eh eh eh! Voila! Ji! Ji! Ji! Voici! Hoh! Hoh! Hoh!")

DUKE: *(From up high.)* Hey, is this your veil?!

ANDREI SEMYONOVICH: Selifan Mitrofanovich! You're being vulgar. They'll think you're an idiot. *(Yells below.)* Madame! C'est le duke. He'll fix you up real nice…

FRANCE: *(Whimpering and kicking her feet.)* Eeeek!

(ANDREI blows her a kiss and the lights go out. The music stops.)

(Silence. Darkness.)

VOICE FROM BELOW: Damnit all! The fuse is blown!

(Suddenly the stage lights up. The stage is bare. AMERICAN, AUNTIE ENGLAND, and FRANCE are all trying to pull out the turnip. POLAND enters the stage. Now the music is playing again. POLAND dances in the middle. The music stops. POLAND stops. She pulls out a large handkerchief and blows her nose into it. She stuffs the handkerchief back into her pocket. Polish folk music begins to play.

POLAND resumes her dance. She stops near the turnip.)

(The music faintly plays.)

DUKE: Andrei Semyonovich, let's get down there! They're going to pull everything out!

ANDREI SEMYONOVICH: Wait, Selifan Mitrofanovich. Let them struggle… and when the turnip comes loose, they'll all fall down. Then we'll bag the turnip! We'll tell them to fuck off!

DUKE: Fuck off!

(Down below: the turnip remains unmoved.)

(They call out for GERMANY. GERMANY enters the stage, dancing. He dances a German dance. He's a little overweight. He falls on all fours and jumps around like a frog in place. The music plays on: "Ach mein lieber Augustin!" Now GERMANY is drinking beer. He approaches the turnip.)

DUKE: *(From up above.)* Tk, tk, tk! Come on, Andrei Semyonovich! We'll go down when the time is right.

ANDREI SEMYONOVICH: We'll bag that turnip!

(ANDREI SEMYONOVICH grabs a bag and DUKE grabs the samovar. They hurry down the stairs. On the right side of the stage, the large book closes.)

(Down below: A CATHOLIC runs on the stage. He dances a Catholic dance. Everyone watches. At the end of the dance, DUKE and ANDREI SEMYONOVICH appear. DUKE holds the samovar under his arm. They get into a line to tug the turnip.)

DUKE: Let's go, let's go, let's go! Come on, guys! Pull! Hey you, over there *(Pointing to the CATHOLIC.)* hold it a little lower! You, America, put some elbow into it! And you, the gangly one over there, grab it by its belly! *(Grunting.)*… Now pull!… Pull! Tk tk tk tk tk.

(The turnip swells and begins to loosen. The music is playing as loudly as possible. The group continues to pull and grunt. Eventually the group, pulling the turnip out of the ground, falls down.)

(ANDREI SEMYONOVICH opens the bag and runs toward the

turnip. Suddenly, a giant Red Army soldier emerges from the turnip. DUKE and ANDREI SEMYONOVICH fall upside-down.)

1935-1938.

THE INTERRUPTION

PRONIN: You have very beautiful stockings.

IRINA: You like my stockings?

PRONIN: I love them!

(PRONIN reaches out to grab them.)

IRINA: What do you like about them?

PRONIN: They are very soft.

(IRINA lifts her skirt up.)

IRINA: Do you see how high they go?

PRONIN: I can see now.

IRINA: And this is where they end. It's all bare leg from here!

PRONIN: And what a leg!

IRINA: I have very fat legs, and very wide hips.

PRONIN: Show me!

IRINA: Oh, I can't do that! I'm not wearing any panties.

(PRONIN kneels down in front of her.)

IRINA: Why are you kneeling?

(PRONIN kisses her leg.)

PRONIN: That's why.

IRINA: *(Giggling.)* Why are you lifting my skirt? I just told you I'm not wearing panties!

(PRONIN continues lifting her skirt.)

Translators' Note: We have adapted this piece from dialogue-heavy short story into play format. Prose between dialogue has mostly been preserved in the form of stage directions.

PRONIN: Shh. Shh.

IRINA: *(Giggling.)* What do you mean, shh?

(Suddenly: a knock at the door.)

(IRINA abruptly pulls down her skirt. PRONIN jumps up and runs to the window.)

IRINA: Who's there?

ANONYMOUS VOICE: Open the door!

(IRINA opens the door. A TALL MAN IN A BLACK COAT and high boots enters. Behind him, a pair of SOLDIERS holding guns enter, with the BUILDING SUPERINTENDENT behind them.)

(The MAN IN THE BLACK COAT approaches IRINA while the SOLDIERS guard the door.)

BLACK COAT: *(To IRINA.)* What's your surname?

IRINA: *(Timidly.)* Mazer.

BLACK COAT: *(To PRONIN.)* And what's your name?

PRONIN: *(Timidly.)* My name is Pronin.

BLACK COAT: Do you have a weapon?

PRONIN: No.

BLACK COAT: *(Pointing to a chair.)* Sit down over there.

(PRONIN sits.)

BLACK COAT: *(To IRINA.)* And you, put on your coat. We're going to need you to come with us.

IRINA: Where? What for?

(Silence.)

IRINA: I'll need to change my clothes.

BLACK COAT: No.

IRINA: I need to put a small something on.

BLACK COAT: No.

(IRINA puts on her coat.)

IRINA: *(Turning to PRONIN.)* Well, goodbye then.

BLACK COAT: Talking is not allowed!

PRONIN: Do I need to come, too?

BLACK COAT: Yes. Put your coat on.

(PRONIN slowly puts on his coat.)

PRONIN: I'm ready.

BLACK COAT: Let's go!

(The SOLDIERS and the SUPERINTENDENT click their heels together.)

BLACK COAT: Get out on the street!

(Exit all.)

(The MAN IN THE BLACK COAT leaves last, slamming the door behind him.)

August 12, 1940.

RATSBY'S VICTORY

CROWD: Hey! Ratsby! Get up!

RATSBY: I'm not getting up.

(RATSBY continues lying on the floor.)

KALUGIN: If you don't get up, Ratsby, I'll make you get up.

RATSBY: I'm not getting up!

SELIZNEVA: Ratsby, all you do is lie on the floor! You're in the way of us walking forwards and backwards!

RATSBY: And I will continue to get in the way.

KORSHUNOV: Well, you know...

KALUGIN: Why are we still talking about this? Someone call the police!

(Someone calls the police.)

(Minutes pass.)

(Enter POLICEMAN.)

POLICEMAN: What's the problem?

KORSHUNOV: Well, sir...

KALUGIN: Here's the problem. All day this citizen lies here, on the floor, getting in the way of our walking forwards and backwards! We've tried to tell him...

SELIZNEVA: We've asked him to go away, but he won't go away.

KORSHUNOV: Right...

(The POLICEMAN approaches RATSBY.)

POLICEMAN: Citizen, why are you lying here?

Translators' Note: We have adapted this piece from dialogue-heavy short story into play format. Prose between dialogue has mostly been preserved in the form of stage directions.

RATSBY: I'm resting.

POLICEMAN: You can't rest here, citizen. Where do you live?

RATSBY: I live right here.

POLICEMAN: Where is your room?

KALUGIN: He's registered to live in this building, sir, but he doesn't have a room.

POLICEMAN: Citizen, where do you sleep?

RATSBY: Right here.

KORSHUNOV: Well…

KALUGIN: He doesn't even have a bed! He just sprawls out across the bare floor!

SUPERINTENDENT: It's true, they've been complaining about him for a long time.

SELIZNEVA: It's impossible to walk forwards and backwards here. We can't keep stepping over him forever! And sometimes he sticks out his leg on purpose. And sometimes… he even sticks out his hand! Then he lies down on his back. He does nothing. He looks at nothing.

KORSHUNOV: Yes, and…

KALUGIN: And he's here all night. We trip over him in the dark. I ripped my blanket because of him!

SELIZNEVA: He lets things fall out of his pockets, too. It's impossible to walk forwards and backwards barefoot, before you even know where you are you've put your foot on something.

SUPERINTENDENT: They tried to light him on fire yesterday.

KORSHUNOV: Well…

KALUGIN: We only poured kerosene to scare him a little, we weren't really going to light him up!

SELIZNEVA: Oh no, we'd never really light a man on fire!

POLICEMAN: But, I don't understand, why is this citizen lying in the hallway?

KORSHUNOV: Like I was saying…

KALUGIN: Because he has nowhere else to live. I live over there. She lives over here. This room belongs to him. So, Ratsby lives in the hallway.

POLICEMAN: That's not good enough. Every citizen should have his own room.

KALUGIN: But there is no other living space except the hallway.

KORSHUNOV: That's what I…

SELIZNEVA: So he lives out here in the hallway!

POLICEMAN: That's not good enough.

(The POLICEMAN exits, shaking his head. The SUPERINTENDENT follows him.)

(KORSHUNOV stands over RATSBY.)

KORSHUNOV: How do you like that, huh!

KALUGIN: *(Approaching RATSBY.)* Did you hear what the officer said? Get up!

RATSBY: I won't get up!

SELIZNEVA: Now he'll never get up!

KALUGIN: *(Angrily.)* Never.

KORSHUNOV: Never.

October or November, 1940.

THE LECTURE

PUSHKOV: What is a woman? A woman is the engine of love.

(Someone runs up and punches PUSHKOV in the face.)

PUSHKOV: What the hell!

(Silence. PUSHKOV continues.)

PUSHKOV: I think you should always approach a woman from underneath. Women love this, they only pretend they don't.

(Again, PUSHKOV gets punched in the face.)

PUSHKOV: What's the problem, comrades! If this is how it's going to be, I won't even talk!

(Minutes pass, and then he continues.)

PUSHKOV: A woman is made to be soft and moist. *(Here again PUSHKOV gets punched in the face. He tries to pretend he doesn't notice, and continues…)* If you just sniff a woman…

(PUSHKOV gets punched so hard in the face that he holds his cheek in pain.)

PUSHKOV: Comrades, I cannot give a lecture under these circumstances! If this happens again, I'm done!

(Silence. Minutes pass.)

PUSHKOV: Now, where were we? Oh, yes, this! Women love to look at themselves. They sit in front of mirrors completely naked…

(Before he can finish his sentence, PUSHKOV gets punched in the face.)

PUSHKOV: Naked.

(He gets punched in the face.)

Translators' Note: We have adapted this piece from dialogue-heavy short story into play format. Prose between dialogue has mostly been preserved in the form of stage directions.

PUSHKOV: Naked!

(Again, he gets punched in the face.)

PUSHKOV: Butt naked! Naked butt and tits!

(Now multiple people are punching him repeatedly.)

PUSHKOV: Tits with an apron!

(More and more punches to the face.)

PUSHKOV: *(Spinning to avoid the punches.)* Asshole of a tart! A naked nun!

(Finally, PUSHKOV is knocked out. He falls to the floor, unconscious. The punches don't stop.)

1940.

MAKAROV AND PETERSEN #3

MAKAROV: This book contains all of our desires and how to fulfill them. Read it, and you'll understand the vanity of desire. You'll see how easy it is to fulfill someone else's desire, but how difficult to fulfill your own.

PETERSEN: You preach so seriously! You sound like the Buddha!

MAKAROV: This is a serious book, and requires lofty speech. I take off my hat just thinking about it.

PETERSEN: Do you wash your hands before touching it?

MAKAROV: Yes, the hands must be washed.

PETERSEN: Do you think the feet must be washed, too, just in case?

MAKAROV: That's not funny. It's just rude.

PETERSEN: So what do you call this book?

MAKAROV: This book has a very mysterious name...

PETERSEN: Hee-hee-hee!

MAKAROV: It is called MALGIL.

(*PETERSEN disappears.)*

MAKAROV: Oh God! What's happening? Petersen!

PETERSEN'S VOICE: What happened? Makarov! Where am I?

MAKAROV: Where are you? I don't see you!

PETERSEN'S VOICE: Where are you? I don't see you either!... What are these spheres?

MAKAROV: What should I do? Petersen, can you hear me?

PETERSEN'S VOICE: I can hear you! Tell me what just happened? And what are these spheres?

MAKAROV: Can you move?

PETERSEN'S VOICE: Makarov! Do you see the spheres?

MAKAROV: What spheres?

PETERSEN'S VOICE: Let go of me!.. Let go!.. Makarov!

(Silence. MAKAROV stands trembling. He opens the book.)

MAKAROV: *(Reading.)* Gradually a person loses shape and becomes a perfect sphere. After a person becomes a sphere, all desire is gone.

(Curtains.)

FOUR EXAMPLES: HOW A NEW IDEA DUMBFOUNDS THE UNPREPARED MIND

1.

WRITER: I'm a writer.

READER: I think you're total s_ _t!

(The WRITER stands still, dumbfounded by this new idea. Minutes pass. The WRITER falls down dead.)

2.

ARTIST: I'm an artist.

WORKER: You're absolute s_ _t!

(The ARTIST turns pale as a canvas.
He sways back and forth like a blade of grass.
Suddenly the ARTIST falls dead,
and is carried away.)

3.

COMPOSER: I'm a composer.

VANYA MONEYBAGS: And I think you're—!

(The COMPOSER begins breathing heavily
and falls down dead. He is, unexpectedly, carried away.)

4.

CHEMIST: I'm a chemist.

PHYSICIST: You're just a—!

(The CHEMIST is silent. Minutes pass. He falls to the floor.)

(Curtain.)

SECTION III: SHORTER PLAYS IN VERSE

TEMPTATION

FOUR GIRLS: *(At the threshold.)*
our legs are aching by the door
sisters, ring the bell
climb the hill!
and slip the shirt off your bare shoulders
climb the hill!
and slip the shirt off your bare shoulders

FOUR GIRLS: *(Getting up from the threshold.)*
We were on that threshold
singing songs, but now
don't grieve, girls
we're slipping our shoulders out of their joints

CHORUS:
All four. We're just
slipping our shoulders out of their joints

FOUR GIRLS: *(On the horizon.)*
our arms are four-dimensional
our heads are shacks
turning our eyes to the east
we see a set of delicate tracks
They only go up a couple flights
since the creation of heights
everything will disappear like a plate
and the garden will be plated
We'll rejoice in our Sunday best
we'll be as sunny as showgirls
Climb that hill
and bare your round shoulders
Climb that hill
and bare your round shoulders

FOUR GIRLS: *(Disappearing.)*
GRO-HO-CHA!

COLONEL: *(In front of a mirror.)*
Whiskers, curl! Get in line!
Saber, snuggle up against my side

Comb, comb!
While I, a Russian gentleman,
won't lift a finger. Am I lazy or what?
I don't know myself! Twirl, little spit curl!
Grow down to the dish, beard
I'm off to clink my spurs
and conquer foreign streets

(Enter MAIDEN.)

MAIDEN:
Colonel, are you upset?

COLONEL:
Oh, no. I just slept badly.
And you?

MAIDEN:
I'm upset, alas.

COLONEL:
I'm sorry for you.
But there's hope
that everything will work out
I advise you to have some fun.
Want to go to the forest? There are some weird pines…
Or to the opera perhaps? Then
I'll write for a carriage from England
for a coachman, too. Or I'll buy tickets
and we'll ride the trolley
to see the princess in orange
I know: you're just a kid,
afraid of getting close to me
but I love you…

MAIDEN:
Get away from me you bastard!

(The COLONEL waves his hand and, grinding his teeth, he leaves like pus leaves a pimple.)

MAIDEN:
Ladies! Where are you?! Where are you?!

FOUR MAIDENS: *(Entering, in unison.)*
You called?

MAIDEN: *(To herself.)*
I'm wicked!

FOUR MAIDENS: *(On the windowsill.)*
You don't want us, Elena.
We're leaving. Farewell, sister!

But what a sweet knee you have, Elena,
your little white foot with a little blister
your girlfriends are still standing
there's no space for us to lie down
Climb the round hill
and slip the shirt off your bare shoulders
Climb the round hill
and slip the shirt off your bare shoulders

FOUR MAIDENS: *(Getting up from the windowsill.)*
Our hands were naught
our heads splashed
our greyish skirts fought
with the roomy draft.

CHORUS:
Hey, you there, don't catch cold
from the roomy draft!

FOUR MAIDENS: *(Looking into a microscope.)*
We looked at each other
through a no-good microscope
what was there, we won't say
we're without language now
There was only an old porch
laden with mounds of gold
above the hill ran a river
nearby, a maiden shivered
Then, looking on eagerly
the colonel said
"Climb this hill,
and bare your shoulders

Climb this hill,
and bare your shoulders."

FOUR MAIDENS: *(Have disappeared and gone silent.)*
?BUT WHYYYY?!?

(That's all.)

Dedicated to K.C. Malevich, February 18, 1927, Petersburg, D. Kh.

UNTITLED (DOCTOR MATRON)

A doctor came from far away
without a basket of hats
he rested at the corners
he arrived and was like that.
The doctor's name was Matron.

Matron was a lout
but from the pocket of the lout
a telescope poked out.

Aunt Katya got ill
she does not lie or sit still
and follows the flies
with motionless eyes.
Aunt Katya doesn't laugh
she only cries like a river
we sent for the doctor
he arrived from far away.

DOCTOR MATRON:
After all, misfortune can befall any wretch
in the form of stomach cancer
but the martyr forgets
and bathes in the water
and then since it's inevitable
brave teeth decay
since for the tooth it's inevitable
you require air and prayer
after all, right after some throw-up
the doctor's roused
to insert a club
into the poor bastard's mouse.

AUNT KATYA:
Doctor, instead of a thermometer,
you've stuck an axis in me!
Doctor, you've deceived us!
Doctor-traitor, this is madness!

DOCTOR MATRON:
Perhaps I'll cure your badness.

AUNT KATYA:
I'm sick of this play!
Disappear into the dark wood!

DOCTOR MATRON:
Have you eaten today?

AUNT KATYA:
I won't though I should.

DOCTOR MATRON:
I'll hit you with a brick.

AUNT KATYA:
Make it quick.

DOCTOR MATRON:
I'll hit you with a brick.

AUNT KATYA:
Make it quick.

The pleasant Doctor Matron
went out the six-fingered door
he dumped the apron
and buried his hands in the ground.
He passed the peasant Thomas
he broke into a monastery
he saw the straw in the darkness
and the poor doctor became statuary.

June 6, 1929.

PAPA AND THE OBSERVERS

PAPA:

Were you watching me dance?

LANDLORDS:

We watched for half an hour—
you stumbled into the mirror,
your hands were wrapped in ribbon.

PAPA:

Children, children in our day
we did not dance as the landlords say,
in our day, we did not hide or look away.

LANDLORDS:

Through the teeth of the comb we saw
your dance techniques.

PAPA:

Teach children the sins and dances
of righteous people, let them twirl
around with a boy or a girl
and torment the old man.

Were you watching me bathe?

LANDLORDS:

We watched from inside the shower.
You stood on the roof like a stork
in the rainstorm for hours.

PAPA:

I trust, I trust in the weather vane.
I was bathing a pelican
is what you saw. Now I'm certain
you're all barbarians.

Were you watching me fly?

LANDLORDS:

From your house, we saw you fly.
You were nothing

but a star, circling in the sky.

(That's all.)

June 6, 1929.

UNTITLED (THE SAND)

NIGHTINGALE: *(Rolling in a box.)*
I sang
now I'm a boomerang
and you're sand
your forehead is vast
lean over
the earth is round
in her, more potholes and boreholes
than eagles
you're locked in the ground beneath your friends' heels
you lie in the desert, yellow and real
your little patch is visible from a rainbow
in you, they bake a potato
I've finished singing
it's time to start flying
time to flay an eagle for a casserole
and into the ground grind the eagle gristle
I'm not the only one they'll put in a box.

A LONE BEDOUIN: *(Looking at the flying sand.)*
There flies the Arabian sand
it buries our eyes
hides people Ah wherever
if only this dream would end.

CHOIR OF BEDOUINS & ARCHANGELS:
Eh let's bang on the sand
let's kick around a silly sad!

A LONE BEDOUIN:
The sand flies belly up
and it ate the little bird
and my horse reared
and the poor little bird disappeared.

CHOIR:
Eh let's bang on the sand
let's kick around a silly sad!

(That's all.)

January 4, 1930.

DINNER

(A VOICE speaks. The stage is otherwise empty.)

VOICE:
He kicked the cocker. Ninety minutes.
The fucker leapt up. He was a brute.
The pike walked out. No cookware.
Hello, Kika. There you are.

(Enter KIKA and NADYA.)

KIKA:
Nadya made a pot of coffee
and said to me, "You copy?"
So I replied: wozard
and in came a wizard.

(Enter WIZARD.)

WIZARD:
Give me bread and scissors.
I have a cold, the shivers.
I'm old and grey and bored.
Please get to know my neighbor.

(Enter NEIGHBOR.)

NEIGHBOR:
Hello Kika, you old lug.
Hello Nadya. Give me a mug.
Hello mug. Hello home.
Hello lamp. Hello gnome.

(Enter GNOME.)

GNOME:
In my dream, I saw a bride.
At dawn, I woke and died.
I thought: must be psychosis!

Koka's coming. Here he is!

(Enter KOKA.)

KOKA:

Wind blew. Sun shone.
Birds sang. Years, flown.
He kicked the cocker.
The fucker leapt up.
Then I came to you alone.

ALL IN UNISON:

Let's eat!

(That's all.)

January 24, 1930, Petersburg.

JOY

CAPE AFILEI:

I won't say
how empty chatter differs
from chatter about fluid things
or, even better, about things of a certain type
in which it's possible to see
the source of life, time, and sleep.
Sleep is a bird with sleeves.
And time—a soup that is high, long, and wide.
And life—the leg of time.
But I won't say what I can say about this
and that's how empty chatter differs
from chatter about the source
of sleep, time, and life.
So time is a soup of sorrow,
and life—kindling,
and sleep's a desert and nothing.
Quiet. In chatter
about anything there's desire
to say something.
And so, hiding our legs in facades,
muddy waters reply.
We're happy as gods,
going to our aunt in Altai.

AUNT:

Hello hello
piebald way
don't you want to fasten a whip
of ink to the letters ABCD?
I'm a grandma, you're a kite
I'm a hole, you're a light
that will ignite
in my ear tonight!

CAPE AFILEI:

Don't overthink
but overthank
don't panic

but picnic
everything will overtake a sloe
to eat cookies and the snow.

AUNT:
Well crawl out of your collar
you're a scholar, you're a dollar.

CAPE AFILEI:
And you, aunt, aren't ill
you're a fly-ka on a hill.

AUNT:
Separate and straight and every day
I was drenched in visible joy
although in the Bible there was a flood
it wasn't in mud but in blood.

CAPE AFILEI:
Tell me, the stlak of grition.
Who, they said, are the ringleaders?
Guess the meday in the kiption
or *(Inaudible.)*

AUNT:
I, an old lady without glasses,
can't see a sprout.
I see alfafa on the ass's muzzle
well then, a sprout!

CAPE AFILEI:
Don't be shifty, old woman
don't speak poppycock
I'll show you how to walk
I'll put you away in a locked room
Where's the crudge? And where's the mudge?
Where's the twice-long river Nile?

AUNT: *(Shaking.)*
Oh, people, don't budge
I died of yellow bile.

CAPE AFILEI: *(Reaching for a pencil.)*
Away, away, away
Get out
aunt, river of joy,
lay your pitchfork on the ground!
Have pity on this sailor boy.

AUNT:
You don't bore and you don't lie
in shtrength and esshence see I
you haven't defiled my soul
because boringshness have I.

CAPE AFILEI:
Because boringshness have I.

AUNT:
Eh, I couldn't swallow a fly
but you eat and eat and eat and eat.
Think a little, why
is everything earthly "eep" and "eat?"

CAPE AFILEI: *(Catching on.)*
It's true—eep and eat!
When you sleep, you don't eat,
when you eat, you don't sleep,
when you weep, you retreat,
you retreat and overeat.
But jam isn't a meal
stick the spoon in your mouth, and bleat
"It needs sugar."
Unreal!

AUNT:
You're a proud nomad
full of tenderness, full of bliss.
Come touch my breasts, give me a kiss…
But let's sit down somewhere first.

CAPE AFILEI:
Give me your heart and a petal,
give me a harp and a kettle,

give me your leg and an ax,
give me an egg and some wax.

AUNT:

Lie down and sleep, and dream
there's an elephant walking downstream.
No! Not an elephant, but Dr. Bull,
who, on his horns, carries null,
only it's not down,
not downstream and not a stream,
not a street and not an alley,
not a valley and not a tong,
not a tongue and not an eye—
only you and only I.

CAPE AFILEI:

Ah, I'm so happy and serene,
my aunt, river of joy,
my aunt, plum tree amongst plum trees,
have pity on this sailor boy.

AUNT:

Well, smack me with a little kiss
right on the nipple and in the nostril,
my cherub, my bliss,
get on your knees, come to my side,
and grope me with your eyes,
hands held behind your back.

CAPE AFILEI:

This, aunt—hm!—is a marvelous idea
you've hit upon. You, like Danaë,
look me in the eye, searching for bliss,
you keep saying to me, "I alone, spry,
came from the summit of the Matterhorn
for you—Ugh!—Altai gave you the hobbit,
an obsolete unit of measurement…"

AUNT:

Well hobbits, so hobbits,
well from the summit, so from the summit.
The thing is, I'm nude.

Does another woman love you?

CAPE AFILEI:
Yes, another, and better
and better and cleaner
and fresher and younger!

AUNT:
My god! My god!
My god! My god!

CAPE AFILEI: *(Changing his socks.)*
You yourself understand I am strong,
young, fresh, we're not a match,
I can hit like a hammer,
I exhale and blow out a match.

AUNT:
I myself breathe like a nation.
The phlegm in my chest is mere salivation.
I hit like a machine,
and can cut up a cube in minutes.

CAPE AFILEI:
I see you won't be coerced,
my aunt, river of joy,
my aunt, panorama of the world,
take pity on the sailor boy.

AUNT:
Look—since, weeping, I am
on my knees before you—
I am young as ever—a lamb!—
holding a lyre and a flute.

CAPE AFILEI: *(Jumping with joy.)*
That's the flow of joy!
I'm a ball of wisdom! Ahoy!

November 11, 1930.

WATER COOLER CHAT

KULUNDOV: Where's my cap? Where's my cap?

RODIMOV: A haughty knight sat on my watch.

KULUNDOV: Did I stick it on the back of my head?

RODIMOV: On the other side of night—day, behind day—a sister.

KULUNDOV: Yesterday my cap was on the shelf. Today it was on the cupboard.

RODIMOV:
Once there was a tsar, who strolled along
Nevskii in a three-cornered hat and a raincoat.

KULUNDOV: But where's my cap?

RODIMOV:
And the tsar laughed
when he saw a little car
At the solemn landowner, he laughed!
Then he pushed the tsarina with his umbrella.

KULUNDOV: My hat's in the trash!

RODIMOV:
The tsar preserved
his age-old glory.
Sappho took a drag
blowing smoke.

KULUNDOV:
Huh? What?
Tell me—where's my scarf?

RODIMOV:
The coachman drove.
He drove on the right side of the street.
He shouted to the tsar: "Get off the road
or I'll run you over!"
The tsar laughed, leaning into the tsarina.

KULUNDOV:

The cold hits my throat.
This evening I'll put on some vaporub.

RODIMOV:

And the tsar cried: what a moron!
I'm wearing a jacket of brass,
and the tsarina, a calendar.
You won't crush me so easily,
you won't move the tsarina with sleds.
As proof, we will lie down
directly beneath the tram.

KULUNDOV:

I advise you, self-friend Kulundov,
to put on a wool shirt later.
Don't go into the courtyard, Kulundov,
but give your mom a little kiss.

MOM: *(Entering.)*

No, no, spare me, Kulundov.

RODIMOV:

And so, throwing their hands up to the sky,
the tsar and tsarina laid on the tracks,
and, docile, with their eyes and guns to Kasky,
the tall soldiers guarded the tsar from attack.
The crowd on Nevskii came to a halt.
the police intermittently charged,
while a bird—swift as a thunderbolt—
looked on with wonder, pupils enlarged.
The tsar got up.
The tsarina got up-a.
Everyone sighed.
"Suck it!" said the tsar.
"We won!" the tsarina cried.
Kasky said: "We cling to Russia and caviar!"
The soldiers were moving aside,
when the coachman grabbed a whip
and smacked the tsar and tsarina like cattle.
The tsar drew his sword
and with the cry, "Death to the rascal!"

began to run down Sadovoi.
The tsarina screamed. The Neva roared.
The people agitated, ready for battle.

KULUNDOV:
Well, farewell, mom,
I'm going across the Karpovka.

MOM: Send my regards to your grandfather twice.

KULUNDOV: Will do!

(Both KULUNDOV and MOM walk off, in opposite directions.)

RODIMOV: *(Alone.)*
So, Minister Porishkevich
was once at a ball
where music growled loudly,
and feet fibbed on the floor of the hall.
A woman with bare shoulders
slithered like a sausage in a squall.
A general slapped his bare heels
for kicks—haha!
The tsar laughed at the tsarina,
and pushed her to the window
to jump on either the sparrows
or the stones—whichever—for kicks.
But the tsarina took the scepter in her fists
and poked him in the balls
with the help of a two-headed eagle—for kicks.

HEAD ON TWO LEGS: *(Entering.)*
You're lying, Rodimov.
I was at that party,
ate pineapple stuffed with turkey,
saw colonels in trousers striped with burgundy.
I relish dealing hearts—
when the ace flies towards my nine,
when the whiskers and epaulettes
shine beneath my goblet of fine wine...
When, swarthy and dark-browed,
the princess, who regards the whole world

with a stern gaze, leans into you, like a cloud,
tenderly, as if you were a little bird....
I love, when our host, getting a whiff of dawn,
suddenly puts out the light,
and the guests, drowsy, withdrawn,
sit around, silent and still as dolomite...
When on the street, growing bright,
a pair of breezes fly about,
when the vacant night abates
and the lifeless flames go out...
I love it, Rodimov! There's no salvation!
Salvation is silly words!
All life is Easter Sunday!

RODIMOV: Shut up, you empty head!

ALARIC, A GOTHIC KING: *(Entering.)*
I saw, in the valleys of the Horn,
the river Styx rushing, imperial.
It looked smart and stern,
as if coming from a burial.
Over the mountain, over the valley,
over the water they flew—
sometimes Mara, sometimes Sally,
their golden tails askew.
God regarded the earthly axis.
All sloshed in me like acid,
all shook this bone edifice,
frail without nails.
Then a corridor opened in space,
liquid ammonia shot up like an oak tree,
a vulture looked me in the face—
a guide to nobody.
Look, the soul's the cowl of verse—
only multiply the books, use pseudonyms,
only hit the bull's eye of the universe,
you'll be forgiven a hundred sins.
Well, Rodimov, show me your palm!

RODIMOV: A knight rides across my palms.

ALARIC: You, Rodimov, are a priestess, and I'm your sleepless judge.

KULUNDOV: *(Running in.)* Where's my belt? Where's my belt?

RODIMOV: Once the tsar lay down in a coffin.

ALARIC: I hear a whisper, a knocking, a step.

MOM: *(Running in.)* Lord, save your faithful servant!

RODIMOV: The candle guttered above the tsar.

KULUNDOV: The belt's on me! I'm wearing it!

(KULUNDOV lies down and goes to sleep.)

RODIMOV:
The single god sat in a group of three.
The tsarina cried at the window.
The tsar said: "My palaces
are empty, but I will return."

(RODIMOV lies down and goes to sleep.)

ALARIC: But I'm not scared of the dead.

(ALARIC lies down and goes to sleep.)

MOM: But I'm scared of the dead.

HEAD ON TWO LEGS:
Sleep, Kulundov, sleep at night,
sleep, Earth, beneath our houses
I see a great white cloud
has risen above us
butterflies dream of beavers
sheep sleep beneath a tent
sleep's casket and thought's freezer open at last
I'm spent
the darkness blurs
I see the cowl of verse
I see the lamps and the deep
out of the salty deep
the people lift their umbrellas
into the world of "however"
sleep, Kulundov, sleep, Rodimov

sleep, Alaric, sleep forever.

MOM: Once the tsar lay down in a swamp…

(That's all.)

(MOM lies down and goes to sleep.)

December 13, 1930.

GVIDON

GVIDON:

The goat rejoices,
the river sparkles.
Your vast and impossible
sweet eyes startle.
Your playful look hides
your dark desires—
oh, Liza, you little liar!
Your silence and whimsy
don't bother me.

LIZA:

Once there was a fairy
who lived in the woods
with the bears and the wolves.
One day, joking around
(as they do in storybooks)
she slipped and fell on the rocks.
She called out for me,
but I couldn't move.
I hemmed and hawed.
I couldn't wipe off my paw.
I trembled beneath the pine trees.
It got worse for me
walking in the woods,
my feet blistered quickly.
The fog climbed into my eye,
my soul took off to the sky.

GVIDON:

Pines creak
lindens creak
the air's a fjord
the wind's cardboard
the coat wears out
the spruces shout
snow falls
the lair calls
the horse's whinny

belongs to me
they're bringing a tub
a whip, and a cup
I stand in the gorse
like a horse
the air's a pullover,
the wind's a pushover

(GVIDON lies down and goes to sleep.)

LIZA:

Soon the morning bell will ring—it's time
to go to church with mama. Look: a line
of people are walking in. There's my bench,
in the corner beneath Magdalene.
Look: below her, the shepherdess Eve hurries
to the valley. The priest here has no mercy:
I'm late, so he'll lock me down below
and order me to spin gold into straw,
or maybe he'll have me executed…

I hope Gvidon will come to my rescue.

(Starts sobbing. Enter WITCH.)

WITCH:

What a wondrous stream of tears!
Stop crying, Liza, dear,
we'll run away from the snow drifts
to piles of moss and twigs in the forest.
Together we'll kill a woodpecker-bird
with a flat pebble you'll find in the dirt.
We'll suck his blood,
throw his feathers in mud.
Night will come. In a hollow
together we'll sit. It's warm there.
Dreamless. The eagles doze early.
We fall asleep: hurly-burly.
When you close your eyes,
I'll bewitch you with sighs…
Everyone wakes up. The blowjob night.

Come quick and we'll away.

LIZA:
I'm too scared
to go with you.
I want to be spared.
I want to go home!
But my legs buckle,
my back aches.
Save me, God! *(Begins running away.)*
Forward, forward!

(Exit WITCH. Enter WOODLAND SCARECROW.)

WOODLAND SCARECROW:
Ha ha ha!
Where are you rushing off to?
Thoughts are air.
Rocks are a middle finger.

LIZA: Are you a kind spirit or an evil one?

WOODLAND SCARECROW:
Lie down on the path, you imbecile,
and lift your knees.
Your wondrous ankles aren't visible
from the celestial trees.

LIZA:
This is your home, brute—
a thicket of moss and sticks.
Spare me, venerable saint Augustine!

WOODLAND SCARECROW: Ho ho ho!

(Exit WOODLAND SCARECROW. Exit LIZA.)

GVIDON: *(Waking up.)*
Where am I? Where am I?
Oh, yes… my room… but why…?
Oh! Yes—a dream-idea, like a butterfly…
I see a noble steed
smash a dungeon with his hooves

and race, race through the woods.
I see a forest, an eagle, sheet lightning.
Against the laws of nature, a spear grazes
the clouds. I hear the monastery bell—
the monks at the church on the hill
run to atone for their sins,
to kiss Saint Augustine's dark robe
and forget death and disease…
Then, furtively looking at Liza,
the monks run into the wardrobe.
Hurry, hurry, put on your boots,
and you, Gvidon, run with the monks
and you, Gvidon, run with the monks
faster, faster, go-go-go.

(GVIDON runs off "with the monks." Enter SAINT AUGUSTINE.)

SAINT AUGUSTINE:

Dawn is here
On the flowers
The plump bees buzz
And the earth
Turns on a turtle's shell
So the son turns
Before birth
In his cell
His face, smooth
His navel feeds
His mother soothes
Here the sun rises sideways
Mass is beginning
The ringers walk from the tower
In pairs to pray
The other day
Rain fell before dawn
I'm off to church

(Enter MONKS, in pairs, and the ABBOT.)

MONKS:

A divine messenger is coming
to us, to us,

let's carpet the way to the altar
with canvas for him.
Sing, monks: Virgo Maria.

ABBOT:
Dawn is here.

SAINT AUGUSTINE:
I have come far.
I have climbed many hills.
Now here's the monastery,
and here's the well.
My breath whispers in my breast.
My legs are weak, yearning
to fold beneath me.
My thoughts flee my temples,
my heart doesn't beat.
The earth rises to meet my forehead…
Monks, carry my coffin.

(He falls. He is dead.)

MONKS:
Someone's fallen in the dirt
  O monks
God is great and small
  Hallelujah
Death is monumental
  O monks
God is fierce and gentle
  Hallelujah
Earth and water will disappear
  O monks
But not God and not Death
  Hallelujah

GVIDON: *(Running in.)* And where's Liza?

ABBOT:
Don't worry, young man.
Sit down.
But not here where oil's been spilled.

GVIDON: *(Panting, struggling to speak.)*
What a disaster…
Night-birds smashed the cupola.
While I was running here,
a picture of spring flashed past—
a feathered eagle flapping…

I'm out of breath.

ABBOT: Would you like a smoke?

GVIDON:
Thanks. *(Lights cigarette, takes a drag.)*
It was like this:
in the blue sky, just a banner,
then a brooding eagle flew,
I looked after him in silence
to see where the king of the wind
was headed on his feathery wings,
where his lungs cut the air with a whistle
in the imperial night.
And for a long while his empyrean way
captivated me.
Eagle in the woods,
eagle over the abyss,
the brooding eagle roars…

ABBOT:
Instead of addressing your questions,
I'll answer with a lesson:
a great tragedy befell my brethren.
I heard graveside weeping
and the bell for a christening—
the venerable Saint Augustine
had died.

GVIDON:
When the purple thistle
    has become myth,
when we hear the whistle
    of the scythe,
when the earth is hewn

in two,
then we will look at the moon
and be afraid.
And the only answer—a steel axe
striking a stump.
Night will go, day will come,
and a choir will hum,
then, will awake from slumber—
a dove,
the ocean waves, the skies' thunder,
my love.

ABBOT:

Your sadness is full of bliss,
blue fog and the moon
your birds fly away
toward A B C and D
you ululate bravely
out of your mind,
a wild cry,
the bedrock of thought,
the soul's falcon, the body's lion.
So love from the body's deep
roars up like a flame
and love's burning cedar
waves its banner over
common sense and reason.
Then doubt creeps in
the terrible ditch of the earth's gift,
nature's knife, mayhem's mist,
the stomach's pathogen,
the bloodline of passion,
the river of our knowledge dries up
a herd of deer gallops
across our great skull
filling the air with screams full
of bliss. This is a sin—
the skull will split like grin.

MONK BASIL:

The letter yat

is at the gate—
Should I make it wait?

ABBOT:
No, no, let it in.

LIZA: *(Entering.)*
I was just in the woods
playing hide and seek with fox cubs
flowers waved their heads
swallows flitted across the sky
frogs croaked in the pond
my bracelets jangled
I got hot
I didn't dare undress
there was a barge on the river
on it, a man flying a kite
my heart beat louder and louder
my blood seethed
I crossed myself
and, tearing my delicate dress
stood up, hiding my shame with a hand..
and the short man on the barge
put his hands around his eyes
to get a better look at me
I hung my dress on a branch
and spread my legs, shamelessly.

GVIDON:
Liza, your behavior
is unworthy of your mouth.
They'll institutionalize you,
Vera Yakovlevna Proust.
Don't you want to understand it,
or are you sick of fate?
Explain it to her, abbot.

ABBOT:
I'm neither god nor a judge.

LIZA:
In our time, morals have,

I know, fallen tremendously.

GVIDON:

Stop it, Liza, you're wrong
and acting carelessly.

LIZA:

Gvidon, you are my fiancé—
of all my suitors, you are the one.
I chose you, a master of verse,
and not to make you miserable
every minute, my dear.

GVIDON:

How glorious!
But will you always be like this?

ABBOT:

The sky hasn't shrunk
earth hasn't dissolved
Look: it's after dusk
you can't make out the church cupola
the planets spin, the sea thwacks
Gvidon and Liza
two carriages
await you by the magnolia.

LIZA:

Thank you, abbot, but we'll take one carriage…

(GVIDON and LIZA leave. The ABBOT adjusts a crumpled flower in the garden. On the stage GVIDON's voice is heard.)

GVIDON:

Touch me, by God!

December 17-20, 1930.

HE AND WINDMILL

HE:
Excuse me, how do I get out of here?

WINDMILL:
I don't know. The sound of water confuses me.

HE:
I can see the train tracks.
Where's the nearest stop, please?

WINDMILL:
Under the lime tree.
My father broke his leg there, you see?

HE:
Yippee!

WINDMILL:
By golly!

HE:
And now? Is your father healthy?

WINDMILL:
Oh, yes, he's teaching cows the ABCs.

HE:
Why does he
teach creatures the ABCs?
With what authority?

WINDMILL:
With an ABC book.

HE:
Pointless, pointless…

WINDMILL:
Hold this moth up to your eye.
Wait, are you blind?

HE:
Truly. For I see among a thousand things…

WINDMILL:
Forgive me, but… how many things?

HE:
A thousand things… very large things.

WINDMILL:
You know, in the moth,
and even in the fly,
there are little boxes
stuck behind the eye
and behind the head—like little corks.
Go take a look.

HE:
Go to hell, jerk!
My eyes don't even work!

WINDMILL:
And what's that growing from your boots?

HE:
That's asparagus roots.

WINDMILL:
Try rubbing your eyes from left to right.

HE: *(Rubbing his eyes.)*
Jesus Christ!
I cracked my eye's frame!

WINDMILL:
Truly. The eyes were not given to us as a game.

HE:
Let me kiss you on your thighs, no shame!

WINDMILL:
Get away from me!

HE:

Don't be so rude. I can't even see!
I need to find a way out. What should I do?

WINDMILL:

Oh, by the way, the train doesn't stop here. Too bad for you.

HE:

You're a liar and you're a con!
I'm staying away from you and your lawn!

December 28, 1930.

UNTITLED (HE AND SHE)

HE:

Come and show me where
you scratched your finger
you better put some iodine on it.

SHE:

Yet again you've found a way to advise me
as if I myself didn't know what to do
I used to make inexperienced men dizzy
I commanded them to kiss my toes
in the fluffy snow.
Those who obeyed quickly
loved me linearly
those who were deterred
grew bitter.

HE:

Science wisdom's princess
slam shut the book of joy
and you wisdom's goddess
show the fist of science to the fool.
The schoolboy makes progress
learning science by rote on his bench
but these symbols, this nonsense
our grandchildren too will forget
as bald stones
they will look into holes
as slender foals
they will grow younger as they go
as *chibu-chibu* in us
they will bloom again
as free herds
they will shake the round earth.

SHE:

I know an ancient hymn
Somewhere, there are scattered
mountains of garbage,
but no fountains.

HE:

On the other hand, there's the mom
of our progeny and *chibiren*.

SHE:

Stop! You're showing me sugar
but where's the sweet fruit?

HE:

The quicker we make a fast raft
and sail on the winding river
the sooner we'll dock at the angelic gate.

SHE:

Where?

HE:

Around the corner.

March 11, 1931.

THE WINDOW

SCHOOLGIRL:
I look out the window
and see shelves of birds.

TEACHER:
You should be looking at the bottom of the mortar
and grinding the grains with the pestle.

SCHOOLGIRL:
I can't grind these stones:
Teacher, they're so hard,
my little hand is soft…

TEACHER:
Well, what a princess!
You must research
the latent heat of vaporization—
only that will complete your education.

SCHOOLGIRL:
Teacher, I'm exhausted
by the continuous chain of experiments.
Five days and nights I grind. And for what?
My hands are numb,
I'm parched—
O God, my God!

TEACHER:
Your suffering will soon be over.
Your mind will clear up.

SCHOOLGIRL:
Ah! I've got a crick in my back!

TEACHER:
Make sure the mortar keeps ringing
and the seeds cracking under the pestle.
I see: you've turned green
and crossed your legs.
This is the eleventh such case
I can recall. What a parable!

The poor thing scarcely strains—
and already her little corpse lies stiff.
Ah, I've got a migraine!
While I climbed on the chair
to fix the clock—
she, poor girl, passed away
before she could finish her education.

SCHOOLGIRL:
Oh, dear teacher,
I've grasped the heat of vaporization—
I've completed my education!

TEACHER:
I'm sorry, but I can't hear you,
though I'd willingly listen!
Little girl, you've become immaterial
and can't say anything more!

WINDOW:
I opened abruptly.
I'm a hole in the wall behind blinds.
The soul spills through me.
I'm a vent for enlightened minds.

March 15, 1931.

UNTITLED (MOTHER AND FATHER)

The mother and father gave birth to a son
and a company of aunts rushed in to see him.
The mother was resting in bed,
and the cradle was rocking in time to a hymn.

FATHER:

Gentlemen, behold my son
you can see he's still mangy.

MOTHER:

Father father
don't talk about your son like that
the child's not so bad really
he's barely opened an eye
and doesn't notice anything in the room
and the eye won't go where it should
his ear can't make out music
and only a knock on his bones gets the sound into his skull
so why, roaring father, do you keep hammering away
on the neverending idea of your own son's grossness?

FATHER:

His figure's like a nail
his glance's so frail
look, wife, what a face
like that of a caroling busker
his face is the color of wax
his lips two cracks
always pulling at the nipple
you're really proud of that little cripple?

MOTHER:

Are you sure you're not glad?
You're a glowing dad.

FATHER:

Shut up mangy woman
and rock the cradle.

March 16, 1931.

WATER AND HNYU

HNYU:

Where, oh where
are you going, Water?

WATER:

To the left.
There, around the bend,
stands a tent.
Inside the tent is a damsel.
Her hair is a black net
engulfing her flesh.
A swallow nests on her nose.
Look how she gets up and goes
out of the garden. She walks straight
for the gate.

HNYU:

Where?

WATER:

There,
around the bend,
the Lady Katya walks the lawn
on her moon-like heels.
In her left eye is a bluebell,
and in her right shines the moon-like hills
with her veels and her nills.

HNYU:

With what? How?

WATER:

I spoke in the tongue of water just now.

HNYU:

Oh no, someone's coming.

WATER:

Where?

HNYU:

There.

WATER:

It's the fisherman, Tommy.
His daughter drowned in me,
he's coming to beat me with rocks.
Hurry, let's talk
loud and fast
about the recent past.

FISHERMAN:

I am all alone.
There is only one me.
Branches grow out of me as if from a tree.
My raw hands cannot hold their needles.
When I look into the sea
I weep quickly,
my eyes turn pink.
I sit in my boat and my boat starts to sink.
I run to the shore but the shore collapses in.
I climb onto the oven,
where my grandparents used to dwell,
but the oven crumbles as well.
Oh, fellow fisherman,
tell me: what should I do?

(He notices HNYU.)

Hnyu—is that you?

HNYU:

Yes. I'm here.
And here's my fiancé, Nakandir.

NAKANDIR:

I have to tell you, I love your daughter
and so need your help in this matter
of conquering her virginity.
I am a long way from Buturlinsk,
I force myself on virgins
while they play on the checkerboard.

And, my good fisherman, for your reward
I'll give you floats of cork
and a fishing net of steel.

FISHERMAN:
Thankyee, thankyee!

NADEAN:
Here—catch this penny!

WATER:
What a horrific scene
I'm seeing.
The old man caught a coin between his teeth!
Faster, faster around the bend
my booming song I'll send.

HNYU:
But, Water, do you have to leave?
Don't you love me?

WATER:
Possibly. But your legs are too thin.
I'm leaving. Where's my walking cane?

HNYU:
Don't you like a woman with black braids?

WATER:
Zhyrk, Zhyrk,
lu lu lu
murmur murmur
Glub
Glub
Glub

(That's all.)

March 29, 1931.

UNTITLED (THE GNOSTIC)

GNOSTIC:

I'll beat every man, woman, and child.

ATRUN:

Praise the best maidens brought to us from each house.

GNOSTIC:

I turn my head on all things
not described in our book of Jesus Christ.
If the maidens reveal their naked bodies,
then let the slaves of Satan look upon them.
For my eyes will look upon the young men
standing in the shape of solemn letters
which, together, form a fish.

ATRUN:

There's so little joy in the folds of your haggard face—
didn't your nanny ever smile?
You tremble at the thought of committing a sin,
certain that a sin will send you straight to hell.

GNOSTIC:

Forget about what I think.
The simple tools of the garden, keys and walking sticks,
can't touch our majesty.
We passed through Roman possession
and decorated ourselves with purple and fine linen.

ATRUN:

You think about the atonements of your sins,
while I think about the consciousness of God.
We are doing our deeds with blood.
But your static mind doesn't allow you
to replace human blood with the blood of an ox.
I replace human blood with the blood of a graceful bird.

1931.

THE ARCHITECT

HEELMAN:

Maria!

MARIA:

Who's calling me?
In eight years I haven't heard
a thing—and suddenly—
some repartee!
I hear the rumble of the carthorses
and the smack of the rifle butt at the changing of the guard.
I hear a conversation between two carpenters.
Here, one says, some cheese.
The other, thoughtful: soup and kasha.
I hear motors whirring on the Neva.
I hear the wind slapping walls and roofs in the plaza.
I hear someone's soft whisper: Masha! Masha!
I've lived eight years without hearing voice, birdsong, sonata.
But who's calling me?

HEELMAN:

Maria!
Can you hear me, Maria?
Don't wait—
get down here, open the door!
Maria, I'm faint.
Hurry, hurry and open the door!
In the dark, all men roar.

MARIA:

I can't decide on my own.
My master's an architect.
Ask him—
maybe he'll let you in.

HEELMAN:

Senseless obedience!
Don't you hear the tumult,
the din of an approaching fight,
terrified civilians watching it unfold,

and the cries of the crowd, and a terrible shout,
and weeping, and mourning,
and silent supplication,
and a short shot over the Neva?

MARIA:
You're wasting your words.
What've you got for me—a horse and a sword?
Where would I go from here?
I'm staying.
After all, I've got a fiancé.

HEELMAN:
The duties of marriage
have their own, uh, distinctive zest…
But who, though unafraid,
returns from battle
only to run into the woods wearing camouflage?

MARIA:
Watch out!
The architect's aimed his gun at your chest!

HEELMAN:
Assassin! You're next!

(The ARCHITECT shoots.)

MARIA:
Ah!
The smoke fills the air with bluish rings!

ARCHITECT:
I cleared the way:
it's a fine day,
and the house is finished—behold the stone lord!
He respects the harmony of heights and weights.
Admire and rejoice!
His firm granite forehead, centuries old,
is like armor in the wall.
The roof, girlfriend of violent storms,
spreads across the graceful rows of windows.
The flag shoots into the air.

Praise and glory to the architect!
And the architect is me.

Spring, 1933.

ANDREI SEMYONOVICH AND THE MATHEMATICIAN

MATHEMATICIAN: *(Pulling a sphere from his head.)*
I pulled a sphere from my head.
I pulled a sphere from my head.
I pulled a sphere from my head.
I pulled a sphere from my head.

ANDREI SEMYONOVICH:
Put it back in your head.
Put it back in your head.
Put it back in your head.
Put it back in your head.

MATHEMATICIAN:
No, I won't!
No, I won't!
No, I won't!
No, I won't!

ANDREI SEMYONOVICH:
Well then don't.
Well then don't.
Well then don't.

MATHEMATICIAN:
Well I won't!
Well I won't!
Well I won't!

ANDREI SEMYONOVICH:
Well fine.
Well fine.
Well fine.

MATHEMATICIAN:
So I won!
So I won!
So I won!

ANDREI SEMYONOVICH:

So you won! Give it a rest!

MATHEMATICIAN:

I won't rest!
I won't rest!
I won't rest!

ANDREI SEMYONOVICH:

You may be a mathematician, but you aren't very smart.

MATHEMATICIAN:

Wrong, I'm smart and I know a lot!
Wrong, I'm smart and I know a lot!
Wrong, I'm smart and I know a lot!

ANDREI SEMYONOVICH:

Sure, a lot of nonsense.

MATHEMATICIAN:

Nope, not nonsense!
Nope, not nonsense!
Nope, not nonsense!

ANDREI SEMYONOVICH:

I'm sick of arguing with you.

MATHEMATICIAN:

Nope, you're not sick of it!
Nope, you're not sick of it!
Nope, you're not sick of it!

(ANDREI SEMYONOVICH wrings his fists in frustration and leaves. The MATHEMATICIAN, having stood alone for a few minutes, follows after ANDREI SEMYONOVICH.)

(Curtains.)

April 11, 1933.

UNTITLED (NICHOLAS AND ALEXANDRA)

NICHOLAS II:

I locked the door
so no one can enter.
I'll sit near the window
and observe the movement of planets in the sky.

(He wipes the misty window with his sleeve.)

Planets, you're like the animals!
You, sun, are a lion, lord of the planets,
king of the sky. You're a tsar…
I'm also a tsar,
so we're brothers, us two.
Shine on me through the window,
my heavenly relative.
Let your rays
enter me like arrows.
I'll unfold my arms
and stand like an eagle.
I'll flap my arms and say bye to earth
and fly through air.
Bye earth! Bye Russia!
Bye beautiful Petersburg!
The people throw their hats up,
and the artillery thunders,
and Prince Suvorov rides in full regalia
and Prince Kutuzov follows
and, in a loud bass,
Lomonosov calls the soldiers onto the battlefield
and infantry run among the bushes
and the field marshal rides through the field
and—

ALEXANDRA FEDOROVNA: *(Offstage.)* Kolya, are you in there?

NICHOLAS II: Yes, I'm here. Come in!

ALEXANDRA FEDOROVNA: I can't. You locked the door. Open it! I have something to tell you.

NICHOLAS II: Hold on, I'll open it.

(He opens the door. ALEXANDRA FEDOROVNA enters.)

ALEXANDRA FEDOROVNA:
Did you do something to the window?
Adam Adamich saw something from the courtyard
that gave him a terrible fright...

NICHOLAS II:
Yes, it's true—
I wiped the windowpane.
It was fogged up after the rain
so I thought: I'll wipe it!

ALEXANDRA FEDOROVNA: But you could've called a servant!

NICHOLAS II: I called Mitka, but Mitka didn't come.

ALEXANDRA FEDOROVNA: Then you could've called Baltazar.

NICHOLAS II:
Baltazar just sits in the kitchen
and lusts after women.
But tell me, where's Adam Adamich?

ALEXANDRA FEDOROVNA:
Adam Adamich is in the pink sitting room
talking to Vorobyov.
Vorobyov's daughter Maria
ran away with her fiancé to Tula.

NICHOLAS II:
What're you saying?
This is news.
Who's her fiancé?

ALEXANDRA FEDOROVNA: Stasov.

NICHOLAS II: What! Stasov! But he's a respectable old man!

ALEXANDRA FEDOROVNA: And old people can be quick on the draw.

NICHOLAS II:

Yes, it's amazing how the world's made!
Everything dead disappears
and day and night everything living
tries to perpetuate itself
whether it's a rose, a fish, or a man—
Everything, everywhere, for love of the queen!
Oh, Stasov! You're an old man.
Your beard is gray,
the pen trembles in your hand,
your voice has lost its former strength,
your feet have begun to shuffle,
and there are many dishes that give you gas,
but passion still knocks in your heart,
where a sly devil lives.

ALEXANDRA FEDOROVNA:

Adam Adamich is coming here with Vorobyov.
Fix your hair and close your dressing gown.

VOROBYOV & ADAM ADAMICH: *(Entering.)*

Hello!
Hello!
Hello!
Hello!

NICHOLAS II:

Hello!
Hello!
Hello!
Hello!

VOROBYOV:

Leave your personal cares,
the hustle and bustle of countless heirs.
Many minds make little work—
Let's devote our days to state affairs.

October 7, 1933.

UNTITLED (RYABICHKOV AND THE COFFEE POT)

(RYABICHKOV runs in carrying a coffee.)

RYABICHKOV: I wanna drink coffee. Who's with me?

ANNA: Is that real coffee?

CHORUS:
Coffee, coffee expands
Expands our will
The coffee drinker understands
Understands our lot

RYABICHKOV: Where's the sugar?

CHORUS:
Sugar Sugar
melts in the flames
Sugar Sugar
horse's reins

HORSE: I'm ready to move in with sugar. Why not?

ANNA: Horse, come take this sugar cube from my hand.

(The horse licks the sugar off ANNA'S hand.)

HORSE: Ah, how tasty, how sweet!

RYABICHKOV: Where's the milk?

CHORUS:
The milk's in the jugs—eight ounces
milk's a pastime for goats
in the snowy, tender mountains
milk shakes the frost from their throats
and the milky ice
slices our throat
and the frost is terribly painful
it cuts you, then numbs you
even beasts perish in the cold…

lock the door tighter!
so the cold won't break in
through keyholes and cracks
we shiver, we're in bed on our backs
already we don't need the lamps
there's darkness around the darkness
we're lambs
we'll perish together
no light. Just yearning all around.

ANNA:
Well, sit down and drink
the fragrant, viscous, lush coffee
so tender and plush.

CHORUS:
We can't, we're in yearning.

RYABICHKOV: And where, missus, is the silver teaspoon?

MISSUS: *(Formerly ANNA.)* The teaspoon melted. It was lying on the stove, and it melted.

CHORUS:
All silver things
trench coats, trench coats
you can buy wax and strings
at the shop near the moat.

1933.

THE BALL

CHORUS:
Dance, dance!

GUESTS:
We're dancing, we're dancing!

CHORUS:
Dance the figure eight!

GUESTS:
We're dancing the figure eight!

CHORUS:
Lock those hips,
Lock those hips,
Now pop,
Pop and pop.

GUESTS:
We're happily locking and popping!

BARONESS PIROGOVA:
I'm suffocating in here.

SOLDIER FERZEV:
Would you like to cool your feverish body on the veranda?

BARONESS PIROGOVA:
You're right: I'm sweating a tiny bit.

(They walk out onto the veranda. BARONESS PIROGOVA holds her arm up into the wind.)

I'll let the wind blow in through my sleeve.

SOLDIER FERZEV:
Look: what a night!

DER GOLDBERG:
Who wants something jolly—
I'll sing no worse than Pavarotti.

HOST:

Ivan Antonich, bring me a whip.
Now Der Goldberg will sing.

(DER GOLDBERG sings. As he sings, the host whips him—one lash for every word.)

DER GOLDBERG:

Love, love
prevails each time...

I won't sing anymore—
He's whipping me!

MARIA:

Oh, look, who's that crawling
toward us on all fours?

HOST:

That's Mothman.

MOTHMAN:

Yes, it's me. A great blow has befallen me
I've become an animal.
Permit me to appeal to the people.

HOST:

Not now. Later, later.

MOTHMAN:

Then I'll withdraw.

HOST:

No, stay. I'm afraid.

MOTHMAN:

This fear's completely unjust.
I'm leaving with slippers of blown dust.

HOST:

Look: he's crawling back.

(MARIA gestures wildly at MOTHMAN.)

JACK:

Maria, be careful.

(MARIA spills wine on JACK.)

MARIA:

I've stained your jacket.

JACK:

Oh, well. It doesn't matter.

MARIA:

My dear Jack...

(MARIA puts her hand on his face.)

JACK:

I'm devoted to you because of your tenderness.

MARIA:

Oh, Jack... Sit there and tell me a story.

JACK:

The sky was dark and stormy. There was thunder.
Suddenly a shot—bang!—from Port Arthur harbor.
On the steamship, hustle and bustle:
The sailors are climbing onto the boat,
The boat's up to here with muscle.
The sailors, wild with fear, drink vodka till they're soaked—
One chops down the mast, one drowns without a whimper,
one with a broken leg lies there and shivers.
Water's already filled the hold,
and people are crazed, trying to stay afloat.
A swell felled a sailor
who called out "Come, come,"
not to the wave, not to anyone—
and he kicked, frantic, in the breakers.
The deep is already sucking him in,
the cold water caresses him,
but there's a man—way out ahead—who swims...
Who releases the darling tide from his fist...
"Come, come!"—to someone he babbles,
to someone he violently burbles,

to someone he tenderly gurgles,
he calls for someone and blathers.

HOST:
That door over there leads to the courtyard.

IVAN ANTONICH:
What're you talking about?

HOST:
Oh, neither this, nor that.

IVAN ANTONICH:
Let's bring out the cards.

MOTHMAN:
I wouldn't say no to a game.

HOST:
Don't lie to me!
You said you were leaving. Get out!

SOLDIER FERZEV: *(Running in.)*
Shoot! Hold! Rib! Kohl!

HOST:
What's this shouting? What's the alarm?
Not even the toe of that criminal will enter my salon!

SOLDIER FERZEV: *(Pointing to the BARONESS PIROGOV.)*
She licked me,
then pricked me,
then kicked me.
She tricked me.

1933.

UNTITLED (THE STUDENT)

FAKIROV:

My soul hurts.
Everything is as it was before,
but there is new life in books.
Still, I don't have time to finish a page
before I hear the telephone ring
and a voice:
    Pyotr Nilich, lunch at Hvalischevskii's today at three. Will you be there?
Yes, I say, I'm there.
And I throw the book aside
and put on my best pair,
I'll be leaving my little cell,
my table, my guitar, my chair.
So I'll shave, put on my best tie,
and walk to the bus stop,
where, just yesterday, after buying new socks,
I ran into Olga Pavlovna, a terrible chatterbox,
and, for 90 minutes, I had to listen to a story about missing keys,
about how her husband, who has no pants, makes them out of cotton hankies,
about Verochka in green knickers,
and Matvei with his devilish grin and black whiskers.
And all my life, every minute,
I wait for wisdom, I save up and I covet,
sometimes I stare at the date with wonder,
sometimes I place letters close together, one after another,
sometimes I mix baking soda with zinc,
sometimes I torment water with a whisk,
sometimes I try to examine electricity with a microscope,
sometimes I repeat all these experiments in an overcoat.
On my own, I made it to the biquadratic equations,
and, sitting in my room, I knew the deer's springtime bucks,
on my own, with my own hand,
I caught a molecule.
That's what I am!

(He pulls a complex machine out of a cupboard.)

And on my own, I constructed this
out of barley.
Who will inspect my machine?
Whose wisdom surpasses my own?

(He ponders this for a minute.)

I carried my "Diverse World" project to the Academy,
but it was overcast, muddy, and lightly drizzling,
and a great misfortune befell me:
the paper got soaked in the rain,
reading it was a big pain;
and no one at the Academy could be bothered to read it.
So today I'm going to Hvalischevkii's.
He bought himself an organ.
We'll listen to Sebastian Bach and drink tea with cloudberry jam.
Where's my cane?
And my other sock?
Found 'em.
Let's go.

(He exits, rolling a cigarette. VEROCHKA runs onto the stage.)

VEROCHKA:
All I want to buy,
all I want
and forget daily
is a jar of interpretation.
The stores don't carry it.
My household's
a knife
to the heart.
Life's a lie.
It's better to lie down, better to die.

(Doorbell rings.)

I have to get the door.

(She runs off. A STUDENT peeks out from the cupboard.)

STUDENT: Ah, Verochka! How I love you!

(He returns to the cupboard. VEROCHKA enters with ANTON ANTONOVICH.)

ANTON ANTONOVICH:
It's a pleasure to see you.
You're gorgeous, Vera.
Trust me: I'm a connoisseur of beauty.
May I call you "Verochka," cutie?

VEROCHKA:
Without wine, Anton Antonovich,
you may only call me "Vera,"
and only kiss my hands
without touching my face.

ANTON ANTONOVICH:
Vera! Verochka! Cutie-pie!
Don't push me away!

(ANTON ANTONOVICH pulls VEROCHKA toward him and pushes his crotch against her.)

VEROCHKA: What the hell is that?

ANTON ANTONOVICH: What? A pipe!

VEROCHKA: Get off me!

(He holds her tighter, grasps her face between his hands.)

ANTON ANTONOVICH:
I can't breathe.
Vera! Verochka! Kiss kiss!

VEROCHKA: Get away! I bite!

ANTON ANTONOVICH: There's no need. Don't be angry!

(He lets her go. She rearranges her hair. A couple minutes pass.)

VEROCHKA: *(Quietly.)* Did you bring chocolate?

ANTON ANTONOVICH:
Sorry. Guilty as charged.
Coming to see you, I was seized by love's ardor

and forgot about everything on earth.
Only you appeared to me many times
in different poses and looks,
with a blouse and without…

VEROCHKA: Ach!

ANTON ANTONOVICH: Without a blouse, your chest…

VEROCHKA: Guard! Save me! People!

STUDENT: *(Jumping from the cupboard.)* Stop, scoundrel! Release her hand! *(Grabs her other hand.)* Don't worry, Verochka. Come join me in the cupboard.

VEROCHKA: Let me go! Who are you exactly?

STUDENT: I'm a student.

VEROCHKA: What do you want from me? Why'd you hide in my cupboard?

ANTON ANTONOVICH: What do you want?

VEROCHKA: Why're you sticking your nose into my personal affairs?

ANTON ANTONOVICH: Are you spying on us?

VEROCHKA: Who are you, really?

STUDENT: I'm a student.

VEROCHKA: And how did you end up here?

STUDENT: I came to see Pyotr Nilich Fakirov.

VEROCHKA: Well?

STUDENT: Pyotr Nilich likes to have an audience whenever he speaks. He puts me in a cupboard and walks and talks as if there were no one in the room.

VEROCHKA: So, while we were here, you were also here?

STUDENT: Yes.

VEROCHKA: And you heard everything?

STUDENT: Yes.

(VEROCHKA covers her face with her hands.)

ANTON ANTONOVICH:

This is an absolute disgrace.
Nowhere to hide, spies everywhere.
My love has reached new heights;
It's too big for the heart-hive.
I have no more power
to conceal my passion-tower.
I'll retreat from the world in a park.
Alone, I'll lie in the grass in the dark,
and there, love, like an angel, will arrive,
and I, a wild boar, will bite my lice-infested hind.
Then a river will rush through me,
and, at the pace of an old geezer,
I'll rush to the appointed place,
where my bride awaits.
My pace will turn to stone
and my hands turn young again.
And my heart leaps, and my gaze begins to burn.
I'm shaking all over.
Oh god! My god!

VEROCHKA:

Ah, stop it! At your age
it's shameful to chase girls.
Your words are like water,
and cannot excite us.
You're toothless! It's gross.
You're half-bald and old
and can't even hold your own breath.

STUDENT:

I have come to this house for four years,
and every day I watch you, Verochka, from the cupboard.
I'm a physicist, studied mechanics,
the free sliding of bodies
and mass attraction, and I've come here only for you.

1933-1934.

PYOTR AND BATOV

PYOTR:

Hey, Batov!
Let's catch a bat!

BATOV:

I don't think I'm ready for that.
Let's catch a cat!

UNTITLED (THE TELEGRAM)

VOSTRYAKOV: *(Looks out the window onto the street.)*
I look out the window and see snow.
My soul's well-acquainted with such wintry scenes.
There's a dumb bro
standing in the entrance to the house opposite.
He holds a stack of books under his arm.
He smokes a pipe with a copper arm.
Now he's started to cross the road
with large, swift strides.
Now he's disappeared.

(Knock on the door.)

Now I hear a knock on the door.
Who's there?

VOICE AT THE DOOR: Open up. Telegram.

VOSTRYAKOV:
He's lying. I can tell he's lying.
There's no telegram.
My heart's writhing—
to open or not to open?

VOICE AT THE DOOR: Open up! What're you waiting for?

VOSTRYAKOV:
Hang on!
Just slide the message under the door.
The lock's broken. *(To audience.)* I should've thought of this before.

VOICE AT THE DOOR:
You need to sign for it.
C'mon, just open the door.
You've got nothing to fear.
Open up! I'm no animal!

VOSTRYAKOV: *(Opening the door.)* Come in. Where are you? What's going on? *(He looks behind the door.)* Where did he go? He couldn't have gone far. There's nowhere to hide. Where'd he go? The street's completely empty. My god! And there're no prints on the snow! So no one came to my door. Who knocked? Who spoke to me through the door?

(He closes the door.)

1937-1938.

ACKNOWLEDGMENTS

We thank Genevieve Arlie, Melody Nixon, Micah Perks, Kylan Rice, Kirill Ulianov, Kelsi Vanada, Kirsten Wagner, G.C. Waldrep, Ronaldo Wilson, Svetlana Stepanova Wimber, Willard Wood, and Karen Tei Yamashita for their support and guidance in making this book.

We are also grateful for fellowships provided by the Iowa Writers' Workshop, the University of California, and Bucknell University, which gave us the time and financial support necessary to complete this translation.

We acknowledge that this translation would not be possible if not for the work of scholars and translators of Daniil Kharms who have come before us. We are particularly indebted to: Anthony Anemone, Ilya Bernstein, Alexander Cigale, Branislav Jakovljevic, Eugene Ostashevsky, Peter Scotto, and Matvei Yankelevich.

Finally we are thankful to our editor, Tyler Crumrine, and everyone at Plays Inverse for helping this book come into the world.

C DYLAN BASSETT is the author of *The Invention of Monsters / Plays for the Theatre* (2015). A graduate of the Iowa Writers' Workshop, he currently teaches creative writing at the University of California, Santa Cruz.

EMMA WINSOR WOOD has a B.A. in Russian History and Literature from Harvard University and an M.F.A. in poetry from the Iowa Writers' Workshop. She edits *Stone Soup*, the literary and art magazine for kids, and teaches writing in Santa Cruz.